Nancy J. Thomas
EDITOR

KNITTER'S MAGAZINE

INSTRUCTION PROOFER
Mary Lou Eastman

BOOK EDITOR
Elaine Rowley

ART DIRECTOR
Bob Natz

PRODUCTION
Kellie Meissner
Jay Reeve
Lynda Selle

PUBLISHER
Alexis Xenakis

KNITTING EDITOR
Ann Regis

PHOTOGRAPHY
Alexis Xenakis

DIGITAL CONSULTANT
David Xenakis

PRODUCTION CHIEF
Carol Skallerud

Second printing 2008,
First published in the USA by
XRX, Inc., PO Box 965
Sioux Falls, South Dakota
57101-0965

ISBN10: 1-893762-00-9
ISBN13: 978-1-893762-00-8
Produced in Sioux Falls, SD
by XRX, Inc. 605-338-2450
Printed in the United States
of America.

Our second afghan is the culmination of a six-part series in Knitter's Magazine that ran over one and a half years with four squares per issue. Each designer featured was given several balls of yarn and basically no restrictions other than size and border. Their unique ideas will astound you and encourage you to build on your knitting knowledge and learn new techniques.

Tips 1 Don't think of all of these squares as equals. Some are fairly simple and others are a bit more challenging. We are presenting all 24, but you need not make an exact copy of our original. You could decide to knit your afghan by repeating several of your favorite squares, or even by making it entirely with one square. As a matter of fact, it's too late to show you all our un-sewn-together attempts, but we thought we could remind you of the many possibilities, by showing our afghan mirror-image on the cover. For a glorious, not-quite-life-sized view of our final arrangement, see pages 26 & 27.
2 Use the squares to come up with other projects. One square with an edging makes an ideal pillow. Back it with a plain square or a second afghan square. With more than 24 squares, you'll have a bedspread; with fewer squares, you can make a baby-sized crib blanket.
3 Due to the nature of the various patterns, all squares may not block to an exact 12" square. As you can see from our sample, when joined they average out.
4 Refer to Knitter's School illustrations (on page 52) to assist you with methods that may be unfamiliar to you.

Needle sizes Most designers used size 7 (4½mm). Some used 6 and 8 (4 and 5mm). Use the size necessary for you to get the given gauge.

Borders Most squares begin and end with three ridges (6 rows) of garter stitch (knit every row) and have a three-stitch garter border at each side edge.

Yarn Patons Décor is sold through fine quality, well stocked yarn shops throughout North America, by Patons Yarns, P.O. Box 40, Listowel Ontario N4W 3H3, or Patons Yarns, P.O. Box 435, Lockport N.Y. 14094. The seven colors in the following chart have been used throughout. Each square takes approximately one ball. Squares with additional colors use small amounts of a ball.

Finishing Pin square to 12" and steam, without placing the iron directly onto piece.

Assembly Sew squares together using grid shown here, fudging a bit if necessary. Use a strand of the most prominent color of the two squares you are joining. We found it less visible to sew the side garter edges together from the wrong side.

YARNS

Patons Decor
75% acrylic, 25% wool
3½oz (100g);
210yd (192m);
19 wraps/inch

#1602 Aran
12 balls

#1631 Taupe
5 balls

#1632 Rich Taupe
2 balls

#1645 Pale Country Pink
3 balls

#1647 Burgandy
3 balls

#1646 Country Pink
4 balls

#1636 Sage Green
2 balls

Susan Levin K53	Rita Garrity Knudson K53	Pam Allen K55	Lyn Youll K54
Charlotte Morris K55	Deborah Newton K55	Rick Mondragon K51	Michele Wyman K55
Debbie New K53	Leigh Witchel K50	Kathleen Power Johnson K52	Jean Frost K52
Gitta Schrade K50	Susan Guagliumi K52	Elise Duvekot K52	Gloria Tracy K50
Lois Young K54	Sue Flanders K50	Linda Cyr K53	Shirley Paden K51
Gayle Bunn K54	Anna Zilboorg K51	Zabeth Loisel Weiner K51	Stephanie Gildersleeve K54

SQUARE SIZE
12" x 12"

AFGHAN FINISHED MEASUREMENTS
4' x 6'

The 5 easiest squares

Deborah Newton
Michele Wyman
Jean Frost
Susan Guagliumi
Lois Young

The 5 most challenging squares

Charlotte Morris
Debbie New
Leigh Witchel
Linda Cyr
Zabeth Loisel Weiner

Susan Levin
VENTURA, CALIFORNIA

I learned to knit from my mother when I was about seven and made doll clothes (primarily scarves) and various gifts of potholders and other simple square (sort of) items that my relatives accepted graciously.

I started knitting again in college and then put in some serious knitting time when I had a long commute to a job in New York City. Unfortunately, when my corporate days ended and "mommy-hood" began, I put my knitting aside as I spent my free time making Halloween costumes, decorating a series of old houses, baking cookies, and volunteering.

When I returned to the corporate world about 15 years ago, I picked up knitting again, not because of a long commute this time, but because I desperately needed a creative outlet. I began taking classes and attending conventions and met Gloria Tracy who encouraged me to design and take my knitting seriously. Three years ago, I again escaped from corporate life and Gloria and I started our own business, K1,C2, (short for Knit One, Crochet Too) which manufactures and markets patterns, yarn, and creative accessories to needleworkers. We both feel fortunate to be using the skills we learned in our "previous lives" as corporate "worker-bees" in a creative, rewarding industry that we love.

Making and giving a Great North American Afghan is truly a labor of love—a love of knitting and love for the lucky recipient. I thought at least one square should be an expression of that love, so I designed the "Heart of My Heart" square. It is made up of two of my favorite kinds of knitting: mosaic and cables. I designed the mosaic part using hearts as the theme and then complemented the hearts with an XO cable design which I remember using so often as a child to represent hugs and kisses.

Since mosaic knitting is most effective when done in garter stitch, the gauge is very different than the stockinette cables. I compensated for the different gauges by using a short-row technique for the mosaic panel, so the center panel ends up with twice as many rows as the outer cable panels and border.

YARNS
A #1631 Taupe
1 ball
B #1647 Burgandy
½ ball

NEEDLES
Size 8 (5 mm) *or size to obtain gauge*

EXTRAS
Cable needle (cn)
Stitch markers

GAUGE
18 sts and 52 rows to 4" (10cm) in Mosaic chart pat

Mosaic chart notes
1 Each chart row consists of k sts and sl sts (or just k sts). Sts to be knit each row are indicated at the right of chart; all other sts in row are slipped purlwise with yarn at WS of work. **2** Each chart row is worked twice, once on RS; then on WS, knitting or slipping the same sts. **3** Work 4 rows of Mosaic chart for every 2 rows of Cable chart. Wrap 1 st at each side of Mosaic chart on every B row to prevent holes (these sts do not appear on chart).

Square
With A, cast on 56 sts. Work 3 ridges, dec 1 st on last row—55 sts. **Beg charts: Row 1** (RS) With A, k3, place marker (pm), work row 1 of Cable chart over 10 sts, yarn back (yb), pm, join B, with yarn forward (yf), sl 1, yb (1 st wrapped), work row 1 of Mosaic chart over 27 sts, yf, sl 1, yb (1 st wrapped), pm. Turn work. **2** Yf, sl 1, work row 2 of Mosaic Chart, yb, sl 1. Turn work. **3** With A, k1, work row 3 of Mosaic chart over 27 sts, k1, work row 1 of Cable chart over 10 sts, pm, k3. **4** With A, k3, row 2 of Cable chart, k1, row 4 of Mosaic chart, k1, row 2 of Cable chart, k3. Cont as established, working 4 rows of Mosaic chart for every 2 rows of Cable chart and garter st border, and wrapping 1 st at each side of Mosaic chart every B row, through row 128 of Mosaic chart. With A, work 3 ridges, inc 1 st on first row. Bind off 56 sts. ∩

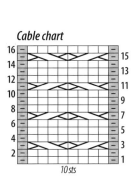

IN OTHER WORDS

2/2 RC Sl 2 to cn and hold to back, k2; k2 from cn.

2/2 LC Sl 2 to cn and hold to front, k2; k2 from cn.

CABLE CHART *OVER 10 STS*

Rows 1, 5, 9, and 13 (RS) P1, k8, p1. *2 and all WS rows* K1, p8, k1.
3, 15 P1, 2/2 RC, 2/2 LC, p1. *7, 11* P1, 2/2 LC, 2/2 RC, p1. *16* Rep row 2. Rep rows 1–16 for Cable chart.

Mosaic chart

27 sts

Cable chart

10 sts

Stitch Key
☐ K on RS, p on WS
⊟ P on RS, k on WS
⤬ 2/2 RC
⤬ 2/2 LC

Color Key
☐ Taupe (A)
■ Burgandy (B)

Rita Garrity
GOLDEN VALLEY, MINNESOTA

A German pharmacist taught me to knit on December 6, 1984, and I have been knitting ever since. I love everything about knitting and find it to be the most enjoyable craft I have ever tried.

I graduated from North Dakota State University School of Pharmacy in 1982. My husband, Dean, and I lived in Washington, D.C., and Baltimore, before settling in the Minneapolis/St. Paul area in 1988. I work part-time as a pharmacist in a Children's Hospital. Dean and I have a five-year old son Thomas and six-month old twins, Jack and Mary.

I wanted my square to be knit circularly. I started with the outer perimeter and worked my way toward the center. A square is created by decreasing at four evenly-spaced points. I wanted to use most of the colors used in the Great North American Afghan. I love gingham and decided to offset the square with it. The colors reminded me of roses so I graphed a rambling rose pattern to frame a bullion stitch rose.

YARNS
MC #1602 Aran
½ ball
A #1631 Taupe
small amount
B #1632 Rich Taupe
small amount
C #1645 Pale
Country Pink
small amount
D #1647 Burgandy
small amount
E #1646 Country
Pink
small amount

NEEDLES
Size 7 (4™ mm) circular,
16" (40cm) long
or size to obtain gauge
Five size 7 (4½mm)
double-pointed
needles (dpn)

EXTRAS
Tapestry needle

GAUGE
20 sts and 28 rows to
4" (10cm) in St st

Notes
1 See *School,* p. 52 for ssk, S2KP2, M1, and duplicate st.
2 Change to dpn when necessary.

Square
Note Work chart rnds 20–29 with MC only (work rambling rose pat in duplicate st after square is completed).
With circular needle and MC, cast on 240 sts. Join and work in rnds as foll: **Rnd 1** *Work rnd 1 of chart over 60 sts; rep from* 3 times more. Cont in pat through chart rnd 45—8 sts. Cut yarn, leaving a 6" tail. Draw tail through rem sts and pull tog tightly. Fasten off.

Finishing
Duplicate st rambling rose pat on rnds 20–29, foll chart. Using photo as guide, use bullion st and work rose in center of square, starting with D, then working outward with E, then C.

Leaf
MAKE 2 WITH A AND 2 WITH B
Cast on 3 sts. Work 12 rows of Chart B. Fasten off last st. Using photo as guide, sew leaves on dec sts around bullion rose. ⌒

IN OTHER WORDS
S2KP2 Sl 2 sts tog knitwise, k1, p2sso.

CHART A *BEG ON 240 STS*
Rnd 1 With MC, *p59, k1; rep from* 3 times more. *2* Knit. *3* P1, *p57, S2KP2; rep from* 3 times more. *4* K1, *k55, S2KP2; rep from* 3 times more. *5* *P55, k1; rep from* 3 times more. *6* K1, *k53, S2KP2; rep from* 3 times more. *7* K1MC, *[k2A, k2MC] 12 times, k2A, k1MC, S2KP2; rep from* 3 times more. *8* *K2A, k2MC; rep from* around. *9* K1B, *k1B, [k2A, k2B] 12 times, S2KP2; rep from* 3 times more. *10* K1B, *[k2A, k2B] 11 times, k2A, k1B, S2KP2; rep from* 3 times more. *11* *K2MC, k2A; rep from* around. *12* K1MC, *k1MC, [k2A, k2MC] 11 times, S2KP2; rep from* 3 times more. **Note** Work rem rnds with MC only. *13* K1, *k43, S2KP2; rep from* 3 times more. *14* *P43, k1; rep from* 3 times more. *15* K1, *k41, S2KP2; rep from* 3 times more. *16* P1, *p39, S2KP2; rep from* 3 times more. *17* Knit. *18* P1, *p37, S2KP2; rep from* 3 times more. *19* K1, *k35, S2KP2; rep from* 3 times more. *20* Knit. *21* K1, *k33, S2KP2; rep from* 3 times more. *22* K1, *k31, S2KP2; rep from* 3 times more. *23* Knit. *24* K1, *k29, S2KP2; rep from* 3 times more. *25* K1, *k27, S2KP2; rep from* 3 times more. *26* Knit. *27* K1, *k25, S2KP2; rep from* 3 times more. *28* K1, *k23, S2KP2; rep from* 3 times more. *29* Knit. *30* P1, *p21, S2KP2; rep from* 3 times more. *31* K1, *k19, S2KP2; rep from* 3 times more. *32* *P19, k1; rep from* 3 times more. *33* K1, *k17, S2KP2; rep from* 3 times more. *34* P1, *p15, S2KP2; rep from* 3 times

Knudson

more. **35** Knit. **36** K1, *k13, S2KP2; rep from* 3 times more. **37** K1, *k11, S2KP2; rep from* 3 times more. **38** Knit. **39** K1, *k9, S2KP2; rep from* 3 times more. **40** K1, *k7, S2KP2; rep from* 3 times more. **41** Knit. **42** K1, *k5, S2KP2; rep from* 3 times more. **43** K1, *k3, S2KP2; rep from* 3 times more. **44** Knit. **45** K1, *k1, S2KP2; rep from* 3 times more.

CHART B *BEG ON 3 STS*
Note Sl sts purlwise with yarn at WS of work.
Row 1 (WS) P3. **2** [K1, M1] twice, k1—5 sts. **3** P2, sl 1, p2. **4** K1, M1, k3, M1, k1—7 sts. **5, 7** P3, sl 1, p3. **6** K7. **8** K1, ssk, k1, k2tog, k1—5 sts. **9** Rep row 3. **10** K1, S2KP2, k1—3 sts. **11** P3. **12** S2KP2.

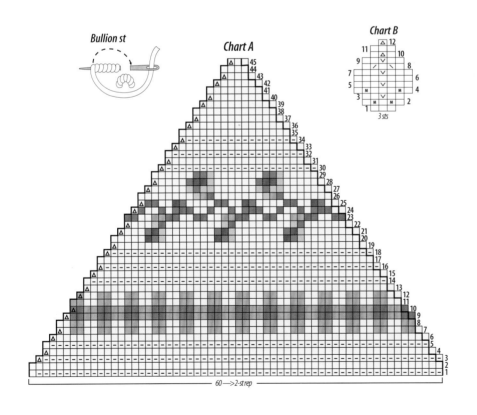

Bullion st

Chart A

Chart B

60 —>2-st rep

**Chart A
Stitch Key**
☐ Knit
— Purl
△ S2KP2

**Chart B
Stitch Key**
☐ K on RS, p on WS
M M1
∨ Sl1 purlwise with yarn at WS
◣ Ssk
◢ K2tog
△ S2KP2

Color Key
☐ Aran (MC)
▨ Taupe (A)
▨ Rich Taupe (B)
☐ Pale Country Pink (C)
▨ Burgandy (D)
▨ Country Pink (E)

Pam Allen
CAMDEN, MAINE

Knitting is what I do. It's what I do when I'm working and what I do when I'm not. I love all the obvious parts— the colors, the textures, the feel of the yarn as I work, the sense of my hands knowing what to do on their own. But also I love the less obvious parts of knitting like problem solving. I enjoy making graphs (on my computer) and drawing schematics. I like pondering problems of fit, the geometrics of armholes and necklines. I respond to patterns or ornaments by thinking—how could I knit that? I delight in meeting fellow knitters. I love knitting traditions and innovation. I still marvel over all the myriad ways things take shape and expression by simply making a loop on a needle. I knit for publication, teach, and develop swatches for the industry. I have two teenage children and would like to find a way to safely knit while driving them from place to place!

My square is somewhat of a surprise. I had no idea that working slipped-stitch in the round (or square) would create a crocheted "granny square" look. One of the reasons I like to work with slipped stitches is that I find it hard to predict exactly what they will look like when knit. You can't chart a slipped-stitch pattern in the same way that you can Fair Isle or intarsia. It's perfect for spontaneous, experimental knitting—you can forget planning and forethought. It's fairly mindless since you use only one color per row—no carrying yarns. And once you get the hang of it, the patterns often invent themselves. One benefit of using slip stitch is that it draws up, like garter stitch, making it possible to increase on every other round and get a piece that lies flat.

YARNS
A #1631 Taupe
½ ball

B #1632 Rich Taupe
½ ball

C #1647 Burgandy
small amount

D #1646 Country Pink
small amount

E #1645 Pale Country Pink
small amount

NEEDLES
Five size 7 (4½mm) double-pointed needles (dpn) *or size to obtain gauge*
Size 7 (4½mm) circular, 24" (60cm) long

EXTRAS
Stitch markers

GAUGE
20 sts and 26 rows to 4" (10cm) in St st

Sl knot circular cast-on
FOR AN EVEN # OF STS
Make a sl knot loop with the cut tail rather than the ball end (Fig. 1). Work into loop as foll: *yo, k1; rep from* until desired even number of sts has been cast on (Fig. 2).

Square
With A, cast on 8 sts using sl knot circular cast-on. Divide sts evenly among 4 dpn. Join and work in rnds as foll: **Rnd 1** *Work rnd 1 of chart over 2 sts; rep from* for each dpn—16 sts. Cont in pat through chart rnd 51. With A, bind off all sts purlwise.

Finishing
Block square. Pull cut tail from cast-on to tighten center, and secure. ∩

IN OTHER WORDS
Yo inc K1, yo, k1 into corner st (2 sts inc'd).
K1b K1 in row below st on LH needle.

CHART *BEG ON 2 STS*
Notes
1 Rep instructions for each dpn. **2** Change to circular needle when necessary, placing markers between reps. **3** Sl sts purlwise with yarn in back.
Rnd 1 With A, k1, yo inc. **2** P2, k1, p1. **3** With B, k2, yo inc, k1. **4** P3, k1, p2. **5** With C, sl 1, k1, sl 1, yo inc, sl 1, k1. **6** Sl 1, k1, sl 1, k3, sl 1, k1. **7** K4, yo inc, k3. **8** With A, k10. **9** P5, yo inc, p4. **10** K12. **11** With B, sl 1, k3, sl 1, k1, yo inc, k1, sl 1, k3. **12** Sl 1, p3, sl 1, p2, k1, p2, sl 1, p3. **13** With C, k2, sl 1, k3, sl 1, yo inc, sl 1, k3, sl 1, k1. **14** K2, [sl 1, k3] 3 times, sl 1, k1. **15** K8, yo inc, k7. **16** With D, [sl 1, k3] twice, sl 1, k1, [sl 1, k3] twice. **17** With B, [sl 1, k3] twice, sl 1, yo inc, [sl 1, k3] twice. **18** K20. **19** K10, yo inc, k9. **20** With E, [sl 1, k1] 11 times. **21** [Sl 1, k1] 5 times, sl 1, yo inc, [sl 1, k1] 5 times. **22** With A, [k1, sl 1] 12 times. **23** K12, yo inc, k11. **24** With C, [sl

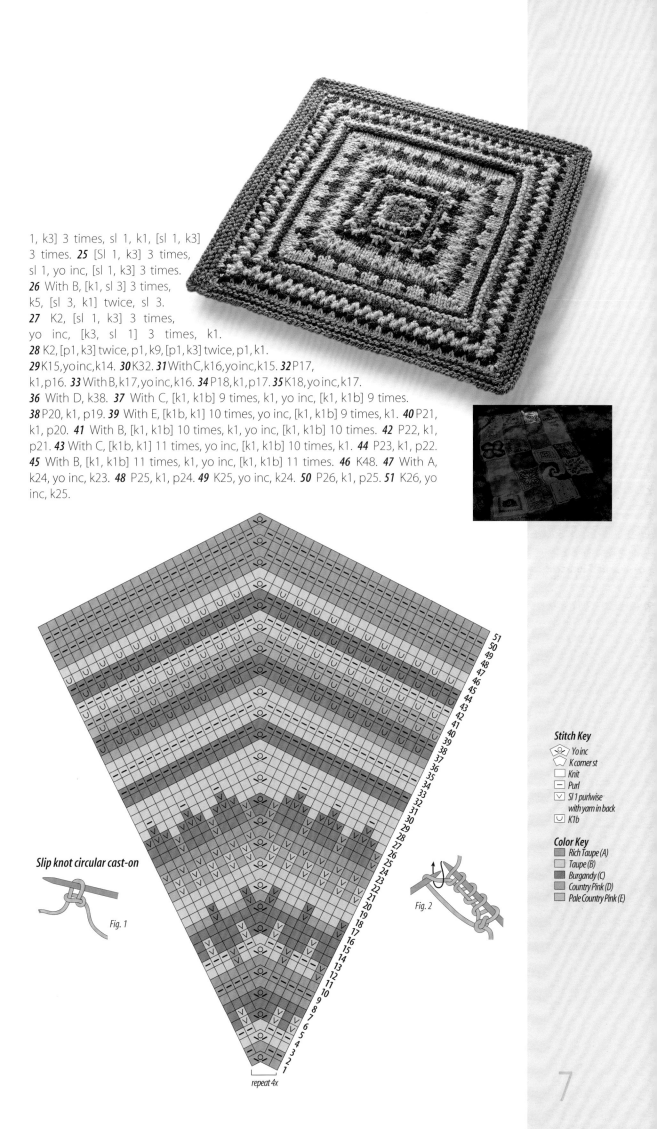

1, k3] 3 times, sl 1, k1, [sl 1, k3] 3 times. **25** [Sl 1, k3] 3 times, sl 1, yo inc, [sl 1, k3] 3 times. **26** With B, [k1, sl 3] 3 times, k5, [sl 3, k1] twice, sl 3. **27** K2, [sl 1, k3] 3 times, yo inc, [k3, sl 1] 3 times, k1. **28** K2, [p1, k3] twice, p1, k9, [p1, k3] twice, p1, k1. **29** K15, yo inc, k14. **30** K32. **31** With C, k16, yo inc, k15. **32** P17, k1, p16. **33** With B, k17, yo inc, k16. **34** P18, k1, p17. **35** K18, yo inc, k17. **36** With D, k38. **37** With C, [k1, k1b] 9 times, k1, yo inc, [k1, k1b] 9 times. **38** P20, k1, p19. **39** With E, [k1b, k1] 10 times, yo inc, [k1, k1b] 9 times, k1. **40** P21, k1, p20. **41** With B, [k1, k1b] 10 times, k1, yo inc, [k1, k1b] 10 times. **42** P22, k1, p21. **43** With C, [k1b, k1] 11 times, yo inc, [k1, k1b] 10 times, k1. **44** P23, k1, p22. **45** With B, [k1, k1b] 11 times, k1, yo inc, [k1, k1b] 11 times. **46** K48. **47** With A, k24, yo inc, k23. **48** P25, k1, p24. **49** K25, yo inc, k24. **50** P26, k1, p25. **51** K26, yo inc, k25.

Slip knot circular cast-on

Fig. 1

Fig. 2

repeat 4x

Stitch Key

⬠ Yo inc
⋀ K corner st
☐ Knit
▭ Purl
⊽ Sl 1 purlwise
　　with yarn in back
⊍ K1b

Color Key

▢ Rich Taupe (A)
▢ Taupe (B)
▢ Burgandy (C)
▢ Country Pink (D)
▢ Pale Country Pink (E)

7

Lyn Youll
TORONTO, ONTARIO

I was born in England and was taught to knit by my grandmother, an avid knitter, when I was very young. I studied for my Bachelor of Arts in Fashion and Textiles. After school, I trained in the art of writing knitting patterns at the UK Patons Yarn Company.

I've been designing for 20 years for yarn companies and book publishers. My work has appeared in magazines in England, Canada, and the US as well as on the stage at the Royal National Theater in London, and even in a Disney movie. Most recently, after working for some time at Patons in Canada, I've decided to return to school. I'm now studying for my Masters of Divinity at Wycliffe College in Toronto.

I've made my home in North America, but sometimes I dream of living in a little cottage somewhere in England. In this afghan square I was able to combine my love of knitting and embroidery with my little dream cottage. I hope that you enjoy knitting it as much as I did!

1/1 RT K2tog, leave on LH needle, k first st again, sl both sts off needle.

Notes
1 See *School*, p. 52 for ssk, intarsia, and duplicate st
2 When working chart rows 3–16 and row 47, carry colors across WS of work; on rows 21–40 and 48–72, use separate balls of yarn for each block of color.
Square
With MC, cast on 58 sts. Work 2 ridges, end with a WS row. Keeping first and last 3 sts in garter st, work center 52 sts in Chart pat through row 74. With MC, work 2 ridges. Bind off all sts.
Finishing
With B, work duplicate st window boxes over 9 sts and 2 rows marked at bottom of both windows. Using photo as guide and D and E, work French knot flowers along bottom of fence, in window boxes, and around door. With F, work straight st leaves on flowers. ∩

YARNS
MC #1602 Aran
   1 ball
A #1631 Taupe
   small amount
B #1632 Rich Taupe
   small amount
C #1647 Burgandy
   small amount
D #1645 Pale
   Country Pink
   small amount
E #1646 Country
   Pink
   small amount
F #1636 Sage Green
   small amount

NEEDLES
Size 7 (4½ mm) *or size to obtain gauge*

GAUGE
20 sts and 26 rows to 4" (10cm) in St st

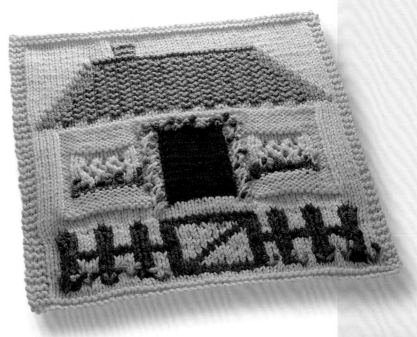

Straight st

French knot

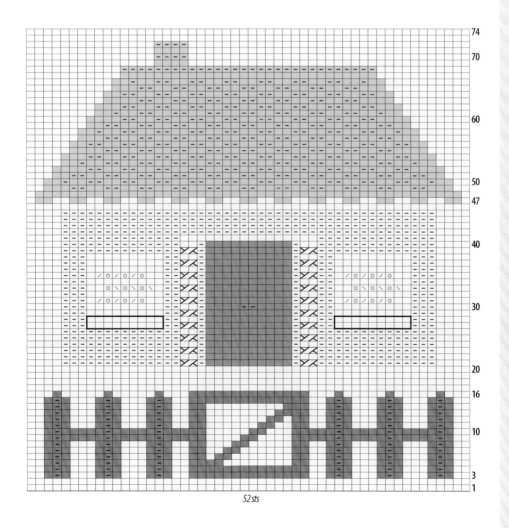

74
70

60

50
47

40

30

20
16

10

3
1

52 sts

Stitch Key

☐ Knit on RS
▨ Knit on WS
╱ K2tog
╲ Ssk
☒ M1L
☒ M1R

Color Key

☐ Aran (MC)
▨ Taupe (A)
▨ Rich Taupe (B)
▨ Burgandy (C)

Charlotte Morris
LOS ALTOS, CALIFORNIA

My mother taught me to knit when I was four and we often sat knitting together, though my bright blue garter stitch squares weren't quite as well made as her sweaters. She knit beautifully even, fine-gauge sweaters, since her wartime childhood in England when wool was rationed and by using a very fine weight you could make a sweater out of a mere four ounces of yarn. I think I owe her for my fondness for fine-gauge knitting. As a child I liked to try many different crafts and actually spent most of my time doing needlepoint. Later, while studying art history, I started knitting more, and by the time I graduated it had become my passion—and it still is. I like to use stitches in ways that take advantage of their intrinsic features, like the zigzag of the chevron that became the basis of the design for this square.

The border of my square is worked sideways in garter stitch which increases and decreases, forming a zigzag along the inner edge. Picking up stitches along the zigzags launches you straight into a stockinette stitch chevron with garter ridges, and a three-needle bind-off allows the chevron to turn the corners. I kept the pinks in stockinette stitch dips between the garter ridges to add just a touch of color round the outside, widening towards the center like a starburst.

YARNS
MC #1602 Aran
1 ball
A #1645 Pale
Country Pink
small amount
B #1646 Country
Pink
small amount

NEEDLES
Size 7 (4½mm)
circular, 24" (60cm)
long *or size to obtain gauge*
Five size 7 (4½mm)
double-pointed
needles (dpn)

EXTRAS
Tapestry needle

GAUGE
19 sts and 40 rows to
4" (10cm) over garter
st (k every row)

Notes
1 See *School,* p. 52 for M1, ssk, and 3-needle bind-off.
2 When working Chart B, change to dpn when necessary.

Square
Border
Side 1 With MC, cast on 9 sts. Work Chart A as foll: work rows 1-30 once, then rep rows 17-30 five times more. Work rows 31-46. **Side 2** Work chart rows 47-62 once, picking up sts between garter ridges of rows below as indicated. Work rows 17-30 six times, then work rows 31-46 once. **Sides 3 and 4** Work as for side 2. Fasten off. Sew corner seam.

Center
With RS facing, circular needle and MC, beg at corner seam (see Fig. 1) and *pick up and k5 sts to base of wave, [pick up and k4 sts along side of next wave, 1 st in top, 4 sts to base] 5 times, then 5 sts to corner, place marker—55 sts; rep from* 3 times more—220 sts. Join and work circularly as foll**: Beg Chart B: Rnd 1** *Work 55 sts of Chart B; rep from* 3 times more. Cont in pat through chart rnd 9—188 sts. **Rnd 10** Remove marker, turn RH needle clockwise so that WS of work is facing outwards. Holding both needles in left hand with points facing in same direction, with dpn, use 3 needle bind-off to bind off 4 sts (5 pairs of sts used). Fasten off last st. Turn needle back to regular position. Replace marker. *With MC, M1 at left edge of bind-off seam (see Fig. 2), work chart pat to 5 sts before next marker, sl 5 sts to RH needle, remove marker, turn RH needle as before. With a separate small length of MC and dpn, bind off 4 sts, using 3 needle bind-off. Fasten off last st. Turn needle back to regular position. Cont with main yarn, M1 at right edge of bind-off seam, replace marker; rep from* twice more. Work chart pat to rnd marker, M1 at right edge of bind-off seam—148 sts. Work chart rnds 11-19—116 sts. **Rnd 20** Work as for rnd 10, working chart pat as indicated for rnd 20—76 sts. Work chart rnds 21-31—44 sts. **Next rnd** Remove marker, turn RH needle and bind off 3 sts, using 3-needle bind-off. Fasten off last st. Return needle to regular position and replace marker, sl 3 sts, *sl 4 sts, remove marker, turn needle and with a separate length of MC, bind off 3 sts, using 3-needle bind-off. Fasten off last st. Turn needle, replace marker, sl 3 sts; rep from* twice more—12 sts. **Next rnd** Removing markers as you go, with MC, *insert LH needle from back to front under strand at left of bind-off, k strand tog with next st, k1, sl next st knitwise to RH needle, insert LH needle from front to back under strand at right of bind-off, sl this strand knitwise to RH needle, then insert LH needle into these 2 sts and complete ssk; rep from* 3 times more—12 sts. Cut yarn, leaving a 6" tail. With tapestry needle, thread tail through all 12 sts twice. Pull snug and fasten off. ∩

IN OTHER WORDS

Wrap st and turn (W&T) With yarn in front, sl 1 purlwise, bring yarn to back, sl st back to LH needle, turn work, bring yarn to back.

Chart A

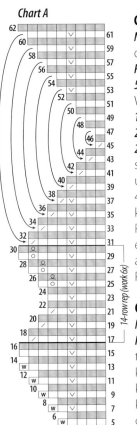

Beg on 9 sts

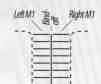

CHART A *BEG ON 9 STS*

Note Sl sts purlwise with yarn in back unless indicated otherwise.

Row 1 K2, W&T. *2 and all WS rows (except 26, 28, 30)* Knit. *3* K3, W&T. *5* K4, W&T. *7* K3, sl 1, k1, W&T. *9* K3, sl 1, k2, W&T. *11* K3, sl 1, k3, W&T. *13* K3, sl 1, k4, W&T. *15* K3, sl 1, k5. *17* K3, sl 1, k3, k2tog. *19* K3, sl 1, k2, k2tog. *21* K3, sl 1, k1, k2tog. *23* K3, sl 1, k2. *25* K3, sl 1, k1, yo, k1. *26, 28, 30* K1, k1 through back loop, k to end. *27* K3, sl 1, k2, yo, k1. *29* K3, sl 1, k3, yo, k1. *31-35* Rep rows 17-21. *37* K3, sl 1, k2tog. *39* K3, k2tog. *41* K2, k2tog. *43* K1, k2tog. *45* K2tog. *47* K1, pick up and k 1 st from end of row 45 (between garter ridges of rows 44 and 46). *Note* On rem RS rows, work to end of row, then pick up and k 1 st (PK1) between garter ridges in rows below, as indicated. *49* K2, PK1 at end of row 43. *51* K3, PK1 at end of row 41. *53* K3, sl 1, PK1 at end of row 39. *55* K3, sl 1, k1, PK1 at end of row 37. *57* K3, sl 1, k2, PK1 at end of row 35. *59* K3, sl 1, k3, PK1 at end of row 33. *61* K3, sl 1, k4, PK1 at end of row 31. *62* K9.

CHART B *55 TO 11-ST REP*

Note Inc 1 by k into front and back of st.

Rnd 1 With MC, p55. *2* With A, k3, [ssk, k2tog, k1, (inc 1) twice, k2] 5 times, ssk, k2tog, k3. *3* With MC, k53. *4* K2, [ssk, k2tog, k1, (inc 1) twice, k2] 5 times, ssk, k2tog, k2. *5* P51. *6* With B, k1, [ssk, k2tog, k1, (inc 1) twice, k2] 5 times, ssk, k2tog, k1. *7* With MC, k49. *8* [Ssk, k2tog, k1, (inc 1) twice, k2] 5 times, ssk, k2tog. *9* P47. *10* See rnd 10 of main instructions, working chart pat as foll: k3, [ssk, k2tog, k1, (inc 1) twice, k2] 3 times, ssk, k2tog, k3. *11* P37. *12* With A, k3, [ssk, k2tog, k1, (inc 1) twice, k2] 3 times, ssk, k2tog, k3. *13* K35. *14* With MC, k2, [ssk, k2tog, k1, (inc 1) twice, k2] 3 times, ssk, k2tog, k2. *15* P33. *16* With B, k1, [ssk, k2tog, k1, (inc 1) twice, k2] 3 times, ssk, k2tog, k1. *17* K31. *18* With MC, [ssk, k2tog, k1, (inc 1) twice, k2] 3 times, ssk, k2tog. *19* P29. *20* See rnd 20 of main instructions, working chart pat as foll: k3, ssk, k2tog, k1, [inc 1] twice, k2, ssk, k2tog, k3. *21* P19. *22* With A, k3, ssk, k2tog, k1, [inc 1] twice, k2, ssk, k2tog, k3. *23, 24* K17. *25* With MC, k2, ssk, k2tog, k1, [inc 1] twice, k2, ssk, k2tog, k2. *26* P15. *27* With B, k1, ssk, k2tog, k1, [inc 1] twice, k2, ssk, k2tog, k1. *28, 29* K13. *30* With MC, ssk, k2tog, k1, [inc 1] twice, k2, ssk, k2tog. *31* P11.

Fig.1

Chart B

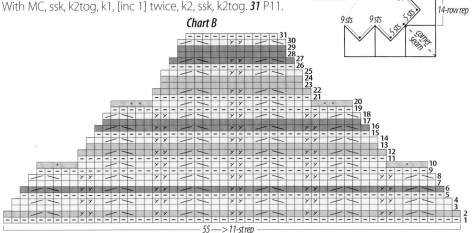

55 → 11-st rep

Chart A Stitch Key

- ☐ Knit on RS
- ▨ Knit on WS
- w W&T
- ▽ Sl 1 purlwise with yarn in back
- ◪ K2tog
- ○ Yarn over
- ⦿ K1 through back loop
- ⌒ Pick up and k 1 st between garter ridges of rows below, indicated by arrow

Chart B Stitch Key

- ☐ Knit
- ⊟ Purl
- ☑ K into front and back of st
- ⟋ K2tog
- ⟍ Ssk
- ▭ See main instructions, rnd 10
- ▭ See main instructions, rnd 20

Color Key

- ☐ Aran (MC)
- ▨ Pale Country Pink (A)
- ■ Country Pink (B)

Left M1 · Right M1 · Bind-off

Fig.2

11

Deborah Newton
PROVIDENCE, RHODE ISLAND

I like everything I design to have at least three elements—a traditional touch, an element of surprise, and something useful. I tried to use these notions even in my afghan square. I've always loved ridged columns, often found in old Gansey sweaters, and incorporated them into this square. And, as an unexpected touch, to add visual interest, I decided to interrupt the columns in two places with a different texture. I tried a totally unrelated pattern—a plain reverse stockinette stitch inserted with eyelets. And, since I'm always using my swatches to test out something new, I tried out a useful buttonhole at the center of my simple cable. In the future, I hope to place this buttonhole cable at the front of a cardigan!

I've been designing knits since 1980 and authored Designing Knitwear (Taunton Press) in 1992. I live and work in Providence with my partner, Paul Di Filippo and my dog Ginger.

Note
See *School*, p. 52 for ssk.

Square
Cast on 55 sts. Work 3 ridges, inc 9 sts evenly across last (WS) row—64 sts. K 1 row. **Beg Charts A and B: Row 1** (WS) K3, then reading charts from left to right, [work 10 sts Chart A, 6 sts Chart B] 3 times, work 10 sts Chart A, k3. **2** K3, then reading charts from right to left, [work 10 sts Chart A, 6 sts Chart B] 3 times, work 10 sts Chart A, k3. Keeping first and last 3 sts in garter st, work charts as established over center 58 sts until 34 rows of Chart A have been worked twice, then work rows 1–7 once more. **Next row** (RS) Knit and dec 9 sts evenly across—55 sts. Work 3 ridges. Bind off. ∩

IN OTHER WORDS
3/3 LC Sl 3 to cn, hold to front, k3; k3 from cn.

Chart A
Rows 1, 3, 5, 7, 9, 11, 13, 15, 27, 29, 31, and 33; (WS) K2, p6, k2. **2, 6, 10, 14, 28, and 32;** P2, k6, p2. **4, 8, 12, 16, 20, 22, 26, 30, and 34;** P10. **17, 19, 23, and 25;** K10. **18 and 24** P2, [p2tog, yo] 3 times, p2. **21** K2, [k2tog, yo] 3 times, k2. Rep rows 1–34 for Chart A.

Chart B
Rows 1, 3, 5, 7 (WS) P6. **2, 6, 10** K6. **4** 3/3 LC. **8** K1, ssk, yo twice, k2tog, k1. **9** P3, k1, p2. Rep rows 1–10 for Chart B.

YARNS
#1631 Taupe
1 ball

NEEDLES
Size 7 (4™mm) or size to obtain gauge

EXTRAS
Cable needle (cn)

GAUGE
22 sts and 30 rows to 4" (10cm) over charts pats

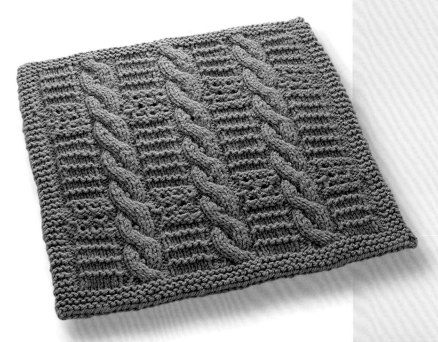

Chart A

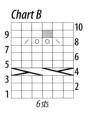

33
32 34
31 32
30
29 28
27 30
26 28
25
23 24
22
21 20
19 18
17 16
15
13 14
11 12
9 10
7 8
5 6
3 4
1 2

10 sts

Chart B

10
9
8
7 6
5 4
3
1 2

6 sts

Stitch Key

- ☐ K on RS, p on WS
- ▨ P on RS, k on WS
- ⟋ K2tog
- ⟋ P2tog on RS, k2tog on WS
- ⟍ Ssk
- ⊙ Yo
- ⟩⟨ 3/3 LC

13

Rick Mondragon
ALBUQUERQUE, NEW MEXICO

I once asked a prominent designer how he judged a design a success. "As long as I like it" was the reply. Although I was taken aback at the time, I believe he made a point. I do believe the design must fit its venue as well. I walk a fine line in designing for publication. I must consider the needs of readers, produce a viable project, and find self-fulfillment in its production.

My teaching and design processes envelop the theory of hidden assets along with the obvious. I try to provide ideas in design, technique, and logic. I want to cheer you to new levels in your knitting and thinking. "You can do it....and more!"

I like classic, wearable silhouettes with creative, unusual, or unexpected elements that make the look interesting and contemporary. The project, its execution, or both require more than just plain knitting. I would say, "The experience has expanded horizons—a new tool for your collection of skills."

My square follows this thinking: Pin stripes in four directions are surrounded and bisected with garter-ridge stripes. It is visually complicated but easily achieved. Circular knitting features a simple cast-on and easy and balanced increases (also mindless). Obvious every-other-row increases and texture are interesting and deliberate. The square would evolve into a fine upside-down raglan for a guy. Fold the square in half for a preview.

The chart and printed words seem intense, yet after 10 quick rounds you'll have experienced all the techniques presented. I find this a clever project for teaching skills— small enough for a knitter to execute and rate for him or herself as usable, likable, and successful!

YARNS
A #1631 Taupe
½ ball
B #1632 Rich Taupe
½ ball

NEEDLES
Five size 8 (5mm)
double-pointed
needles (dpn)
or size to obtain gauge
Size 8 (5mm) circular
16" (40cm) long

GAUGE
20 sts and 30 rows to
4" (10cm) in Chart pat

Notes
1 Take care to hold yarn in a consistent manner throughout.
2 Change to circular needle when necessary

Sl knot circular cast-on
FOR AN EVEN # OF STS
Make a sl knot loop with the cut tail rather than the ball end (fig. 1). Work into loop as foll: *yo, k1; rep from* until desired even number of sts has been cast on (fig. 2).

Square
With A, cast on 16 sts using sl knot circular cast-on. Divide sts evenly among 4 dpn. Join and work in rnds as foll: **Rnd 1** *Work rnd 1 of chart over 4 sts; rep from* for each dpn. Cont in pat through chart rnd 45. With A, bind off all sts purlwise.

Finishing
Block square (it will take some coaxing to lie flat and achieve a 12" square). Pull cut tail from cast-on to tighten center, and secure. ∩

IN OTHER WORDS
Yo inc K1, yo, k1 into corner st (2 sts inc'd).
CHART *BEG ON 4 STS*
Note Rep instructions for each dpn.
Rnd 1 With A, yo inc, k3. **2** With A, purl. **3** With B, k1, yo inc, k4. **4** With B, purl. **5** K1A, k1B, yo inc with A, [k1B, k1A] twice, k1B. **6, 8, 10, 12, 14, 16** *K1A, k1B; rep from* across dpn. **7** K1A, k1B, k1A, yo inc with B, [k1A, k1B] 3 times. **9** [K1A, k1B] twice, yo inc with A, [k1B, k1A] 3 times, k1B. **11** [K1A, k1B] twice, k1A, yo inc with B, [k1A, k1B] 4 times. **13** [K1A, k1B] 3 times, yo inc with A, [k1B, k1A] 4 times, k1B. **15** [K1A, k1B] 3 times, k1A, yo inc with B, [k1A, k1B] 5 times. **17** With B, k8, yo inc, k11. **18** With B, purl. **19** With A, k9, yo inc, k12. **20** With A, purl. **21** With B, k10, yo

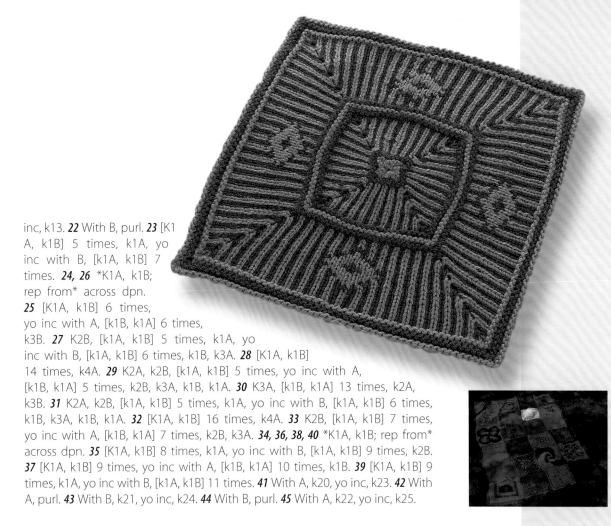

inc, k13. **22** With B, purl. **23** [K1
A, k1B] 5 times, k1A, yo
inc with B, [k1A, k1B] 7
times. **24, 26** *K1A, k1B;
rep from* across dpn.
25 [K1A, k1B] 6 times,
yo inc with A, [k1B, k1A] 6 times,
k3B. **27** K2B, [k1A, k1B] 5 times, k1A, yo
inc with B, [k1A, k1B] 6 times, k1B, k3A. **28** [K1A, k1B]
14 times, k4A. **29** K2A, k2B, [k1A, k1B] 5 times, yo inc with A,
[k1B, k1A] 5 times, k2B, k3A, k1B, k1A. **30** K3A, [k1B, k1A] 13 times, k2A,
k3B. **31** K2A, k2B, [k1A, k1B] 5 times, k1A, yo inc with B, [k1A, k1B] 6 times,
k1B, k3A, k1B, k1A. **32** [K1A, k1B] 16 times, k4A. **33** K2B, [k1A, k1B] 7 times,
yo inc with A, [k1B, k1A] 7 times, k2B, k3A. **34, 36, 38, 40** *K1A, k1B; rep from*
across dpn. **35** [K1A, k1B] 8 times, k1A, yo inc with B, [k1A, k1B] 9 times, k2B.
37 [K1A, k1B] 9 times, yo inc with A, [k1B, k1A] 10 times, k1B. **39** [K1A, k1B] 9
times, k1A, yo inc with B, [k1A, k1B] 11 times. **41** With A, k20, yo inc, k23. **42** With
A, purl. **43** With B, k21, yo inc, k24. **44** With B, purl. **45** With A, k22, yo inc, k25.

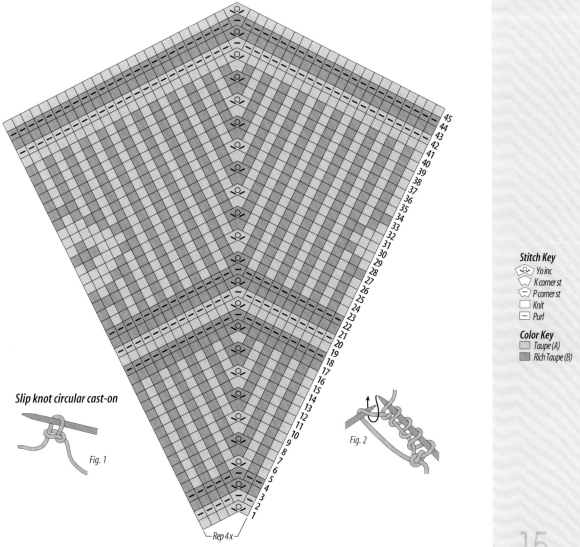

Stitch Key
⚲ Yo inc
⌃ K corner st
⌄ P corner st
☐ Knit
— Purl

Color Key
☐ Taupe (A)
■ Rich Taupe (B)

Slip knot circular cast-on

Fig. 1

Fig. 2

← Rep 4 x →

Michele Wyman
CHANDLER, ARIZONA

My earliest knitting memory is as a lone six-year old, sitting comfortably amidst Philadelphia neighborhood "bubbies"—either 'bubby' who would have me, as one of my grandmothers was a dress designer, the other one was into crochet—and learning knitting basics. My next memory is as a college student knitting afghans to keep me warm during cold Penn State winters and sweaters that always came out too large for the boyfriend of the season. I didn't "get it" about gauge until years later.

After 34 years, with the support of knitting friends and a very supportive local shop owner, I made the leap from avid knitter to designer. This came shortly after a residential change from Philadelphia to El Segundo, California. As I remember it, I decided to put what I had been learning about design into practice while achieving the goal of knitting all my holiday gifts that year.

As math and I were never close friends, I find it ironic that I'm now designing full time. On the other hand, my degree and background are in writing, so the ability to write patterns clearly makes sense. I've had an opportunity to marry my professional background and my passion for knitting to create a wholesale pattern publishing company called Effectiveness by Design. It provides a wonderful balance to my other professions—human resources consultant and single mom.

Whenever I start a new design, my vision is to create a project that only looks difficult (in other words, deceptively easy), has a classic look, and works up relatively quickly. My square is in keeping with that vision and has a bit of a southwest flair—in keeping with my current residence in a suburb of Phoenix, Arizona.

YARNS
MC #1602 Aran
    1 ball
A #1646 Country
    Pink
    small amount
B #1647 Burgandy
    small amount

NEEDLES
Size 6 (4mm) *or size to obtain gauge*

GAUGE
19 sts and 24 rows to 4" (10cm) over Charts A and B

TW2 Sl 1 purlwise with yarn in back, k1; pass sl st over k st and leave it on LH needle; k sl st through back loop and drop from needle.

Square
With MC, cast on 61 sts. Work 3 ridges, end with a WS row. *__Beg Chart A: Row 1__* (RS) K3, [TW2, p3] 3 times, work 25 sts of Chart A, [p3, TW2] 3 times, k3. **2** K3, [p2, k3] 3 times, work 25 sts of Chart A, [k3, p2] 3 times, k3. Cont in pats as established through chart row 26. *__Beg Chart B: Row 1__* (RS) Work 18 sts in pat as established, work 25 sts of Chart B, work in pat to end. Work as established through chart row 14. Work from * to * once. Work 3 ridges. Bind off. ∩

Chart A

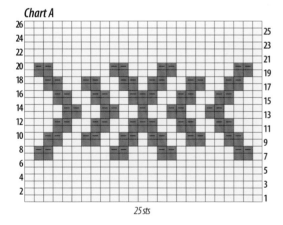

25 sts

Chart B

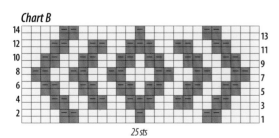

25 sts

Stitch Key
☐ K on RS, p on WS
⊟ P on RS, k on WS

Color Key
☐ Aran (MC)
▨ Country Pink (A)
▨ Burgandy (B)

Debbie New
WATERLOO, ONTARIO

At my school in Australia, we were required to knit a yearly social-service project. In my enthusiastic childhood, I began early and knit a complete lacy layette, but as a teenager I would start the night before the deadline and only knit a pair of booties. This lack of dedication carried me through university and into adulthood when I began knitting again for my family.

I developed a sweater technique which involved doing a long tail cast-on until the tail ran out, then knitting on in rib and Fair Isle until I could see whom it was likely to fit. If it didn't fit anybody, I had another child or adopted somebody. Fortunately I eventually discovered the joys of knitting non-wearable objects which can be any size. I like to avoid the straight line or grid approach to knitting and enjoy designing things which continue to have creative interest for me throughout their construction.

This knotted garter square tames a flowing band by confining it within bounds. It plays with the idea of a garter as a continuous closed ring. Wherever possible I have picked up rather than seamed and have used garter-stitch grafting and three different cast-ons for a uniform effect. You may want to weave in ends as you go as there are a number of color changes. The pattern of colors shown can, of course, be rearranged. A gradation from dark to light to dark gives a pleasing ribbony look.

Garter-stitch grafting is used to complete the outer garter-stitch ridge while sewing together. It joins knitwise to a row of stitches and purlwise to an edge. From the viewpoint of a knitted piece lying face upward, knitwise grafting goes down through one stitch and up through the adjoining stitch leaving a horizontal thread behind the work. Purlwise grafting goes up through a stitch and then down through its neighbor, leaving a horizontal thread on the right side.

YARNS
A   #1602 Aran
    ½ ball
B   #1647 Burgandy
    ½ ball
C   #1646 Country
    Pink
    ½ ball
D   #1645 Pale
    Country Pink
    ½ ball

NEEDLES
Size 8 (5 mm) circular,
24" (60cm) long *or
size to obtain gauge*

EXTRAS
Stitch markers
Tapestry needle
Waste yarn

GAUGE
20 sts and 36 rows to
4" (10cm) in garter st
(k every row).

Notes
1 See *School*, p. 52 for ssk, backward loop cast-on, and invisible cast-on.
2 For ease in working, mark RS of square.

Square
Border
With A, cast on 224 sts. Do not join. **Row 1** (RS) [K2tog, k52, ssk] 4 times—216 sts. **2, 4** Knit. **3** [K2tog, k50, ssk] 4 times—208 sts. Cut yarn, leaving an 8" tail. With RS facing, sl 17 sts to RH needle. ***Beg Center Triangle Chart: Row 1** (RS) Join A and work chart row 1 over 18 sts. Turn work. Work chart row 2 over 16 sts—13 sts. Cont in chart pat through row 14. Fasten off last st. With RS facing, sl next 8 sts to RH needle. **Beg Corner Triangle Chart: Row 1** (RS) Join A and work chart row 1 over 18 sts. Cont in chart pat through row 6. Cut yarn and pull through 2 rem sts. With RS facing, sl next 8 sts to RH needle. Rep from* 3 times more, sewing mitred corner of border (being careful not to twist) before working last corner triangle.

Coil #1
With RS facing and B, leave an 18" tail for grafting later and beg at point AA (see Coil Diagram), **pick up and k14 sts evenly along LH side of center triangle, k8, pick up and k14 sts along corner triangle, k8, pick up and k14 sts along RH side of next center triangle, cast on 6 sts, using backward loop cast-on—64 sts. Turn work**. **Next row** K64, cast on 18 sts, using invisible cast-on—82 sts. **Beg Coil Dec Chart: Row 1** (RS) With B, k10, [place marker, work 12-st rep] 6 times. Cont in chart pat, working rep sts between markers, through chart row 21 (remove markers on last row)—16 sts. Cut yarn, leaving a 15" tail. With WS facing and tapestry needle, thread tail through first 5 sts, sl them off needle and pull tog firmly. With RS facing, graft sts to garter edge, foll Garter Stitch Grafting diagram.

Coil #2

With RS facing and B, pick up and k18 sts evenly along top of Coil #1. Work between **'s of Coil #1—82 sts. **Next row** Knit. Work Coil Dec Chart and complete as for Coil #1.

Coils #3 and #4

Work as for Coil #2, picking up first 18 sts along top of preceding coil.

Finishing

With RS facing, and open sts at bottom, graft rem garter edge to 18 invisible cast-on sts, using garter st graft and 18" tail from beg. Block square. ∩

IN OTHER WORDS

Note St count after bound-off sts does not include st rem on RH needle.

CENTER TRIANGLE CHART

BEG ON 18 STS

Row 1 Bind off 2 sts, k15. *2* Bind off 2 sts, k11, k2tog. *3, 5, 7, 9* K2tog, k to last 2 sts, ssk. *4* Ssk, k7, k2tog. *6, 8, 10, 12* Knit. *11* K1, ssk. *13* K2tog. *14* K1.

CORNER TRIANGLE CHART

BEG ON 18 STS

Row 1 Bind off 1 st, k5, ssk, k2tog, k7. *2, 4* Ssk, k to last 2 sts, k2tog. *3* K2tog, k2, ssk, k2tog, k3, ssk. *5* K1, ssk, k2tog, ssk. *6* K2tog, ssk.

COIL DEC CHART *BEG ON A MULTIPLE OF 12 STS, PLUS 10*

Row 1 With B, k10, *k5, k2tog, k5; rep from*. *2 and all WS rows* Knit with color of row below. *3* With B, k10, *k3, k2tog, k6; rep from*. *5* With C, k10, *k5, k2tog, k3; rep from*. *7* With C, k10, *k1, k2tog, k6; rep from*. *9* With C, k10, *k5, k2tog, k1; rep from*. *11* With D, k10, *k2tog, k5; rep from*. *13* With D, k10, *k3, k2tog, k1; rep from*. *15* With D, k10, *k1, k2tog, k2; rep from*. *17* With A, k10, *k2, k2tog; rep from*. *19* With A, k10, *k2tog, k1; rep from*. *21* With A, k10, *k2tog; rep from*.

GARTER STITCH GRAFTING

Insert needle down into first st, *then under purl bump on garter edge. Bring needle up again into same st as before, then down into next st over; rep from*.

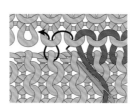

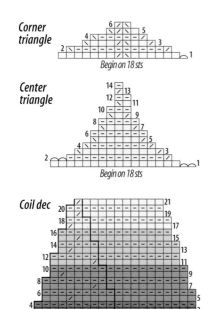

Corner triangle
Begin on 18 sts

Center triangle
Begin on 18 sts

Coil dec
12—>1-st rep

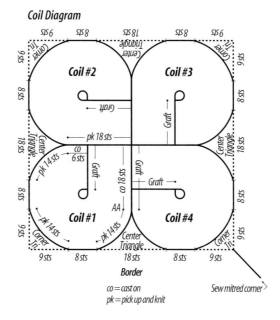

Coil Diagram

Coil #2   Coil #3

Coil #1   Coil #4

Center Triangle

Center Triangle

Corner Tri.   Corner Tri.

pk 18 sts

co 6 sts

pk 14 sts   pk 14 sts

Graft   Graft   Graft

AA   co 18 sts

Center Triangle

Border
9 sts 8 sts 18 sts 8 sts 9 sts
co = cast on
pk = pick up and knit
Sew mitred corner

Stitch Key

☐ K on RS
⊟ K on WS
∩ Bind off 1st
⟋ K2tog
⟍ Ssk

Color Key

☐ Aran (A)
■ Burgandy (B)
■ Country Pink (C)
▨ Pale Country Pink (D)

Leigh Witchel
NEW YORK, NEW YORK

I taught myself to knit in 1989 when I was dancing for American Festival Ballet in Boise, Idaho. My earliest work draws on my own blissful ignorance, and Kaffe Fassett's Glorious Knits explorations of color (my third sweater, a version of Kaffe's "Jack's Back" jacket, looks rather like the roof of a Howard Johnson's after a collision with a Benjamin Moore truck.)

The more I knit, my fascination grew with textures and shaping unique to knitting. The Wedding Cake Square represents my attraction to both sides of knitting, the "Devil may care, break all the rules" side, and the me that likes to know the rules inside out before I break them.

My inspiration for this square came about through the afghan title and the yarn colors. A Great American Afghan, like a Great American Novel, makes me think of a broad scope, and I wanted to use a traditional American needlecraft in an updated fashion. At first I thought in terms of quilting, but didn't like the patchwork swatches I created. I went back to a traditional medallion counterpane and updated it by adding color. But it really took shape when I reviewed the confectionery-cake frosting colors. I began to think of wedding cakes and gifts and decided to knit a cake! In fact, it would make an excellent wedding present if made into a pillow.

This square is active visually, but not difficult. All the colorwork is slip stitch using only one color per row. It is worked from the center out with the central cast-on made easier by knitting a rose and casting on the square from it. I hope these design features will make it as enjoyable to knit as it was to design.

YARNS
A #1646 Country
Pink
½ ball
B #1602 Aran
½ ball
C #1645 Pale
Country Pink
½ ball

NEEDLES
Five size 6 (4mm)
double-pointed
needles (dpn)
or size to obtain gauge
Size 6 (4mm) circular
needles, 16" (40cm)
and 24" (60cm) long

EXTRAS
Stitch markers

GAUGE
20 sts and 28 rows to
4" (10cm) in St st

Notes
1 See *School*, p.52 for M1 and knitting on cast-on.
2 Sl all sts purlwise.
3 Beg Main Square on dpn, changing to circular needle when there are enough sts. For ease in working, place a marker after last st of each dpn before transferring sts.

CENTER ROSE
Petal 1
With A, make a slip knot on one dpn. Cast on 1 st by knitting on—2 sts. Work 15 rows of Chart A. **Row 16** Pick up and k 1 st from straight edge at beg of petal (forming a small circle)—2 sts. **Row 17** K2tog. Do not fasten off.
Petal 2
Cast on 1 st as before—2 sts. Work rows 1–7 of Chart A. Work chart row 8 as foll: K4, with RH needle, pick up and k 1 st from straight edge of previous petal at point as shown on Rose Diagram. Place st on LH needle and k2tog. Work chart rows 9–15. **Row 16** Pick up and k 1 st from straight edge at beg of petal. **Row 17** K2tog. Do not fasten off.
Petal 3
Rep between *'s of Petal 2 once. **Row 16** Pick up and k 1 st from straight edge approx halfway around previous petal (at beg of Petal 4). **Row 17** K2tog. Do not fasten off.
Petal 4
Rep between *'s of Petal 2 once. **Row 16** Pick up and k 1 st from straight edge (where petal 4 ends on diagram). Fasten off, leaving a 12" yarn tail. Draw yarn through loop. Use yarn tail to neaten base of rose with a few overcast sts.
MAIN SQUARE
With RS facing, dpn and B, pick up and k20 sts around base of rose. Divide sts evenly among 4 dpn. Join and work in rnds as foll: **Rnd 1** *Work rnd 1 of Chart B over 5 sts; rep from * for each dpn. Cont in pat through chart rnd 51. Bind off all sts purlwise with A. ⌒

20

IN OTHER WORDS

K1 float Insert RH needle under float 2 rnds below and then knitwise into next st on LH needle; k these 2 tog.

Make bobble (MB) ([K1, p1] 3 times, k1) in a st; pass first 6 sts, one at a time, over first st.

CHART A *BEG ON 2 STS*

Row 1 (RS) K2. **2** K2. **3** K1, M1, k1. **4** K3. **5** K2, M1, k1. **6** K4. **7** K3, M1, k1. **8** K5. **9** K2, k2tog, k1. **10** K4. **11** K1, k2tog, k1. **12** K3. **13** K1, k2tog. **14** K2. **15** K2tog.

CHART B *BEG ON 5 STS*

Note Rep instructions for each dpn.

Rnds 1, 3 With B, knit. **2, 4** With B, yo, k to last st on dpn, yo, k1. **5** With A, knit. **6** With A, yo, p to last st on dpn, yo, k1. **7** With B, knit. **8** With B, [yo, k2tog] 5 times, yo, k1. **9** With A, knit. **10** With A, yo, p to last st on dpn, yo, k1. **11, 13, 16, 19** With B, knit. **12** With C, yo, [k1, sl 5 with yarn in front (wyif)] twice, k1, yo, k1. **14** With B, yo, k4, k1 float, k5, k1 float, k4, yo, k1. **15** With C, yo, k1, sl 4 wyif, k1, sl 5 wyif, k1, sl 4 wyif, k1, yo, k1. **17** With B, yo, k3, [k1 float, k5] twice, k1 float, k3, yo, k1. **18** With C, yo, k1, sl 3 wyif, [k1, sl 5 wyif] twice, k1, sl 3 wyif, k1, yo, k1. **20** With B, yo, k2, [k1 float, k5] 3 times, k1 float, k2, yo, k1. **21** With C, knit. **22** With C, yo, p to last st on dpn, yo, k1. **23** With B, k to last 3 sts on dpn, M1, k3. **24** With B, [yo, k2tog] 14 times, yo, k1. **25** With C, knit. **26** With C, yo, p to last st on dpn, yo, k1. **27, 29, 31, 33, 35, 37, 39** With B, knit. **28** With B, yo, k to last st on dpn, yo, k1. **30** With A, yo, k1, sl 2 with yarn in back (wyib), [MB, sl 1 wyib, MB, sl 5 wyib] 3 times, MB, sl 1 wyib, MB, sl 2 wyib, k1, yo, k1. **32** With A, yo, k1, sl 2 wyib, [MB, sl 3 wyib] 7 times, MB, sl 2 wyib, k1, yo, k1. **34** With C, yo, k1, sl 5 wyib, [MB, sl 3 wyib, k1, sl 3 wyib] 3 times, MB, sl 5 wyib, k1, yo, k1. **36** With A, yo, k1, sl 4 wyib, [MB, sl 3 wyib] 8 times, sl 1 wyib, k1, yo, k1. **38** With A, yo, k1, sl 6 wyib, [MB, sl 1 wyib, MB, sl 5 wyib] 4 times, sl 1 wyib, k1, yo, k1. **40** With B, yo, k to last st on dpn, yo, k1. **41** With A, knit. **42** With A, yo, p to last st on dpn, yo, k1. **43** With B, k to last 3 sts on dpn, M1, k3. **44** With B, [yo, k2tog] 24 times, yo, k1. **45** With A, knit. **46** With A, yo, p to last st on dpn, yo, k1. **47** With B, knit. **48** With B, yo, p to last st on dpn, yo, k1. **49** With C, knit. **50** With C, yo, p to last st on dpn, yo, k1. **51** With A, knit.

KNITTING ON CAST-ON

1 Make a slipknot on left needle. Working into this knot's loop, knit a stitch.

2 Place new stitch on left needle as shown.

3 Insert right needle knitwise into last stitch and knit a stitch and place it on left needle. Repeat step 3 for each additional stitch.

Chart A
Stitch Key

☐	K on RS
⊟	K on WS
◉	M1
⟋	K2tog

Chart B
Stitch Key

☐	Knit
⊟	Purl
◯	Yarn over
⟋	K2tog
⩔	Sl 1 wyif
⩒	Sl 1 wyib
Ⓜ	M1
∪	K1 float
●	MB

Color Key

▨	Country Pink
☐	Aran
▨	Pale Country Pink

Chart B

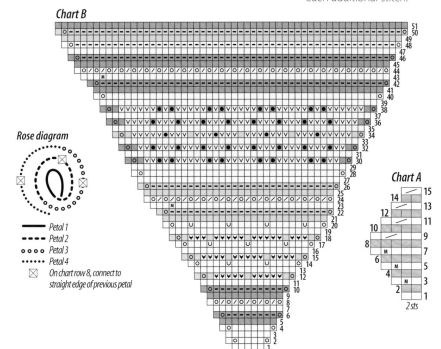

Rose diagram

——	Petal 1
- - - -	Petal 2
∘∘∘∘	Petal 3
········	Petal 4
⊠	On chart row 8, connect to straight edge of previous petal

Chart A

21

Kathleen Power
SARASOTA, FLORIDA

My plan for my life has been not to grow old regretting that I hadn't tried something which interested me. This best describes my career as a writer and fiber artist. While my greatest obsession is handknitting and crocheting, my creative tentacles have reached out to almost all fiber crafts. I gather them in and create hybrids of all that I love best about color, texture, and technique. Every time I fear there isn't much left to learn, I turn an exciting new corner. This energy has produced my fiber art buttons, eclectic crochet, and knit beaded accessories, and fiber art. I design and write articles for yarn companies and magazines. Teaching keeps the creative engine primed so I have taught at Embellishments, Stitches, for the Crochet Guild of America, TKGA, and knitting guilds across the country. I live in Florida with two whippets, more beads than fleas, two knitting machines, and a yarn stash as big as Idaho!

This embossed diagonal counterpane block pattern is a fusion of the simple "Bassett Pattern" in Mary Walker Phillips' Knitting Counterpanes with the intricate embossed effects typical of many counterpane motif designs. Leaves are among the most common embossed details in this knitting genre. For this block, I chose a contemporary lacy leaf to complement the recurring mesh pattern. Bobbles are the real heavyweights in embossed motifs. Here, four-stitch bobbles are grouped at one corner. Picture an actual counterpane where this square would be joined with three others: the bobble clusters would form a dense centerpiece flanked by the delicate leaf elements converging in radiating squares. The lattice-like mesh contributes a delicate overall balance.

I've become fascinated with the rich textural quality of traditional knit medallions as well as the potential for contemporary interpretations. As a puzzle-lover, finding new ways to combine different geometric shapes and stitch patterns is the ultimate challenge in knit design.

YARNS
#1631 Taupe
1 ball

NEEDLE
Size 7 (4½ mm) *or size to obtain gauge*

GAUGE
20 sts and 26 rows to 4" (10cm) in St st

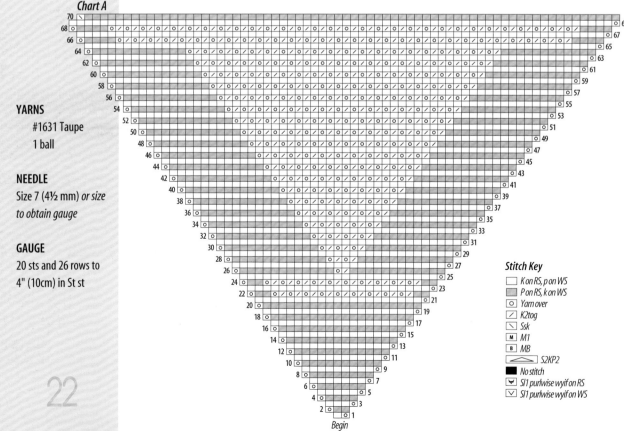

Chart A

Stitch Key

- ☐ K on RS, p on WS
- ▨ P on RS, k on WS
- ○ Yarn over
- ╱ K2tog
- ╲ Ssk
- Ⓜ M1
- Ⓑ MB
- ◁▷ S2KP2
- ■ No stitch
- ⮃ Sl 1 purlwise wyif on RS
- ⮁ Sl 1 purlwise wyif on WS

Begin on 1 st

Johnson

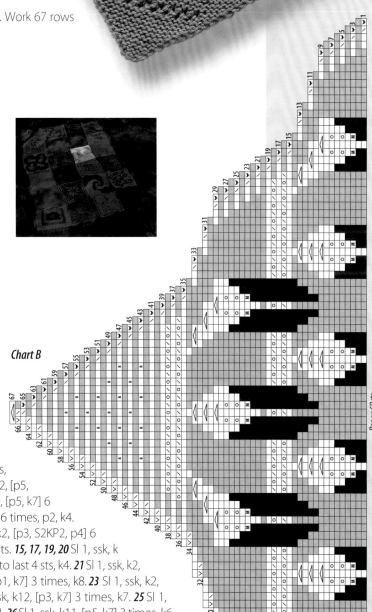

Notes
1 See *School*, p. 52 for ssk, M1, and S2KP2.
2 For ease in working, mark RS of square.

Square
Cast on 1 st. Work 70 rows of Chart A—69 sts. Work 67 rows of Chart B. Fasten off last st.

Finishing
Damp block to 12" square.

IN OTHER WORDS
Make Bobble (MB) K into front, back, front, back of st, turn; sl 1, p3, turn; sl 1, k3, turn; sl 1, p3, turn; sl 2 tog knitwise, k2tog, p2sso.

CHART A *BEG ON 1 ST*
Row 1 (RS) Yo, k1. **2** Yo, k2. **3–21** Yo, k to end. **22, 24** Yo, k2, *yo, k2tog; rep from* to last 2 sts, k2. **23 and all foll RS rows** Yo, k to end. **26** Yo, k12, yo, k2tog, k12. **28** Yo, k12, [yo, k2tog] twice, k12. **30–64** Cont as established, working 1 more [yo, k2tog] in center on WS rows. **66, 68** Yo, k4, *yo, k2tog; rep from* to last 4 sts, k4. **70** Ssk, k to end—69 sts.

CHART B *BEG ON 69 STS*
Note Sl all sts purlwise with yarn in front.
Row 1 (RS) Sl 1, ssk, k2, p9, [k1, p7] 6 times, p3, k4. **2** Sl 1, ssk, k11, [p1, k7] 6 times, k6. **3** Sl 1, ssk, k2, p8, [M1, k1, M1, p7] 6 times, p2, k4. **4** Sl 1, ssk, k10, [p3, k7] 6 times, k5. **5** Sl 1, ssk, k2, p7, [(k1, yo) twice, k1, p7] 6 times, p1, k4. **6** Sl 1, ssk, k9, [p5, k7] 6 times, k4. **7** Sl 1, ssk, k2, p6, [k2, yo, k1, yo, k2, p7] 6 times, k4. **8** Sl 1, ssk, k8, [p7, k7] 6 times, k3. **9** Sl 1, ssk, k2, [p5, k2, S2KP2, k2, p2] 6 times, p4, k4. **10** Sl 1, ssk, k7, [p5, k7] 6 times, k2. **11** Sl 1, ssk, k2, [p4, k1, S2KP2, k1, p3] 6 times, p2, k4. **12** Sl 1, ssk, k6, [p3, k7] 6 times, k1. **13** Sl 1, ssk, k2, [p3, S2KP2, p4] 6 times, k4. **14** Sl 1, ssk, k5, [p1, k7] 6 times—55 sts. **15, 17, 19, 20** Sl 1, ssk, k to end. **16, 18** Sl 1, ssk, k3, *yo, k2tog; rep from* to last 4 sts, k4. **21** Sl 1, ssk, k2, p11, [k1, p7] 3 times, p5, k4. **22** Sl 1, ssk, k13, [p1, k7] 3 times, k8. **23** Sl 1, ssk, k2, p10, [M1, k1, M1, p7] 3 times, p4, k4. **24** Sl 1, ssk, k12, [p3, k7] 3 times, k7. **25** Sl 1, ssk, k2, p9, [(k1, yo) twice, k1, p7] 3 times, p3, k4. **26** Sl 1, ssk, k11, [p5, k7] 3 times, k6. **27** Sl 1, ssk, k2, p8, [k2, yo, k1, yo, k2, p7] 3 times, p2, k4. **28** Sl 1, ssk, k10, [p7, k7] 3 times, k5. **29** Sl 1, ssk, k2, p7, [k2, S2KP2, k2, p7] 3 times, p1, k4. **30** Sl 1, ssk, k9, [p5, k7] 3 times, k4. **31** Sl 1, ssk, k2, p6, [k1, S2KP2, k1, p7] 3 times, k4. **32** Sl 1, ssk, k8, [p3, k7] 3 times, k3. **33** Sl 1, ssk, k2, p5, [S2KP2, p7] twice, S2KP2, p6, k4. **34** Sl 1, ssk, k7, [p1, k7] 3 times, k2—35 sts. **35–40** Rep rows 15–20—29 sts. **41** Sl 1, ssk, k to end. **42 and all foll WS rows** Rep row 41. **43** Sl 1, ssk, k4, [MB, k3] 4 times, k4. **45** Sl 1, ssk, k5, [MB, k3] 3 times, k5. **47** Sl 1, ssk, k2, [MB, k3] 4 times, k2. **49** Sl 1, ssk, k3, [MB, k3] 3 times, k3. **51** Sl 1, ssk, k4, [MB, k3] twice, k4. **53** Sl 1, ssk, k5, MB, k8. **55** Sl 1, ssk, k2, [MB, k3] twice, k2. **57** Sl 1, ssk, k3, MB, k6. **59, 61, 63, 65** Sl 1, ssk, k to end. **67** S2KP2—1 st. ∩

Chart B

Beg on 69 sts

Jean Frost
SAN DIEGO, CALIFORNIA

I'm one of those knitters who began knitting as a child. My childhood diary notes my knitting lessons and progress. My interest in knitting really picked up when I was in high school and began knitting things for "Bundles for Britain" during World War II. This was followed by knitting twelve "sloppy joe" sweaters.

In time my early knitting efforts led to knitting jackets to wear with the skirts I had, and from there to knitting whole suits. I knit suits for all occasions from business to cocktail parties. Eventually this led to designing for yarn companies and magazines.

As I was the only one in my family who displayed a great interest in knitting, I was given the samplers made by my grandmother. This was her way of passing along to her daughters her love of knitting. Unfortunately, they were all interested in crochet. The samplers were beautiful even though they are worked with package string. As she lived a pioneer life far from stores this was all she had to work with. These samplers have sparked my interest in knit items made by pioneers. This past summer, I visited several museums displaying articles made by pioneer women.

This square is based on a coverlet made by a Danish woman. I've never seen I-cord used in this way and was fascinated by the original article which appears to have been worked in one whole piece. Much patience went into producing such a coverlet.

Square
Cast on 56 sts. Work 3 ridges, end with a WS row. Keeping first and last 3 sts in garter st, work center 50 sts in Chart pat through chart row 64. Work 3 ridges. Bind off. ∩

IN OTHER WORDS
2-st I-cord (2IC) *With dpn, k2, do not turn, slide sts to other end of dpn; rep from* 5 times more. Sl sts to RH needle.

CHART *OVER 50 STS*
Rows 1 and 5 (RS) *P2, k2; rep from*, end p2. *2 and all WS rows* K the knit sts and p the purl sts. *3, 7* *K2, p2; rep from*, end k2. *9* P2, k2, p2, k38, p2, k2, p2. *11, 15, 19, 23, 27, 31, 35, 39, 43, 47, 51, 55* K2, p2, k42, p2, k2. *13, 53* P2, k2, p2, k18, 2IC, k18, p2, k2, p2. *17, 49* P2, k2, p2, k15, [2IC, k1] 3 times, k14, p2, k2, p2. *21, 45* P2, k2, p2, k12, [2IC, k1] 5 times, k11, p2, k2, p2. *25, 41* P2, k2, p2, k9, [2IC, k1] 7 times, k8, p2, k2, p2. *29, 37* P2, k2, p2, k6, [2IC, k1] 9 times, k5, p2, k2, p2. *33* [P2, k2] twice, k1, [2IC, k1] 11 times, [k2, p2] twice. *57–64* Rep rows 1–8.

YARNS
#1602 Aran
1 ball

NEEDLES
Size 7 (4½ mm) *or size to obtain gauge*
Two size 7 (4½ mm) double-pointed needles (dpn)

GAUGE
20 sts and 26 rows to 4" (10cm) in St st

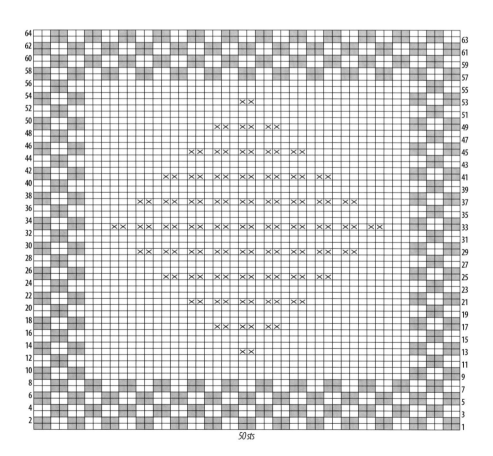

Stitch Key

☐ Knit on RS
▨ Knit on WS
☒☒ 2-st I-cord

50 sts

Gitta Schrade
TORONTO, ONTARIO

My mother taught me to knit when I was six. My mother and grandmother always had at least one knitting project going. Craft was also a part of the daily school routine—knitting, crocheting, sewing, weaving, and cross–stitching. Soon everybody in the family had at least one of my sweaters. I started producing one-of-a-kind sweaters for special customers. When I feel like dropping the knitting needles for a few days, I pick up a crochet hook or tapestry needle.

I moved from Germany to New Zealand where I spent a few years working as a designer and pattern writer. From there I traveled around the United States for a few months and ended up in Toronto where I've been for the past few years. I design and write patterns for yarn companies and magazines. I do translations of patterns as well.

The basic idea for this square occurred to me when I was watching rain finding its way through the flowerbed in front of my window. By looking at something, I can see it in my mind in a different shape, texture, color combination, or proportion. It always translates into something usable for a design. I used traveling cables and I-cords to create this effective, but not difficult afghan square. To achieve an even more interesting piece, vary I-cord sewing positions on several squares.

Note See *School*, p.52 for invisible cast-on and M1.

Square

With size 7 (4½mm) needles and MC, cast on 58 sts using invisible cast-on. Work 69 rows of chart pat. Place sts on hold. With RS facing, circular needle and MC, pick up and k46 sts along left side edge, work across sts of invisible cast-on as foll: Cast on 1 st, place 3 sts of Cable "1" on hold, p9, place 3 sts of Cable "2" on hold, cast on 1 st, p7, place 3 sts of Cable "3" on hold, cast on 1 st, p8, place 3 sts of Cable "3" on hold, cast on 1 st, p7, place 3 sts of Cable "2" on hold, cast on 1 st, p9, place 3 sts of Cable "1" on hold, cast on 1 st, pick up and k46 sts along right side edge, work across sts of chart row 69 as for cast-on edge—184 sts. Join and work in rnds as foll: **Next rnd** [P46, M1] 4 times—188 sts. **Next rnd** With CC, [k46, k into front, back and front of next st (dbl inc)] 4 times—196 sts. P 1 rnd. **Next rnd** K47, dbl inc, [k48, dbl inc] 3 times, k1—204 sts. P 1 rnd. **Next rnd** K48, dbl inc, [k50, dbl inc] 3 times, k2—212 sts. P 1 rnd. Bind off all sts knitwise with MC. Work Cables "1" as foll: Sl 3 sts from holder to dpn. K3, k into st below last st worked—4 sts. Work 4-st I-Cord for 6½". **Next row** [K2tog] twice. **Next row** K2tog. Fasten off. Work Cables "2" in same way, working I-Cord for 1½". Work Cables "3" in same way, working I-Cord for 1". With tapestry needle and MC, sew I-cords in position, using photo as guide. Steam gently without flattening. ⌒

YARNS
MC #1602 Aran
  1 ball
CC #1631 Taupe
  small amount

NEEDLES
Size 7 (4½mm) *or size to obtain gauge*
Size 6 (4mm) circular needle 24" (60 cm) long
2 double-pointed needles (dpn)

EXTRAS
Tapestry needle
Stitch holders

GAUGE
18 sts and 26 rows to 4" (10cm) in St st using size 7 (4½mm) needles

I-CORD

I-cord is a tiny tube of stockinette stitch, made with 2 double-pointed needles.

1. Cast on 3 (or more) stitches.
2. *Knit 3 (or more). Do not turn work. Slide stitches to right end of needle.

Repeat from* for desired length. The tube forms as the yarn is pulled across the back of each row.

Susan Guagliumi
CHESHIRE, CONNECTICUT

For the last 15 years I have traveled the U.S. as a knitting machine educator for several companies, most recently as Education Director for Studio by White. How did I get started? I finished graduate school 17 years ago and there were no jobs for teaching weaving and related textiles. So.... having seen a knitting machine at TNNA (The National Needlework Association) I wrote the company and told them why they needed me to represent them in the northeast. I received two machines via UPS in July and by October was on the road training dealers. I never had the opportunity to be just a knitter—it has always been tied to teaching, and promotion. With my sister-in-law as partner, I opened...have you any wool? in Cheshire, CT three years ago. The shop caters to both hand and machine knitters. My book Hand Manipulated Stitches for Machine Knitters (Taunton) continues to be a machine-knitting classic. I've been married to Arthur Guagliumi, one of my undergraduate college professors, for 29 years. My son, Jordan, comprises the sun, moon, and most of the stars in my sky. We live in an 1832 Greek Revival home and after a dozen years we are nearly through with renovation.

Twisted stitches are first cousins to 1 X 1 cables, but do not need a cable needle to hand knit; by machine they utilize a pair of two-prong transfer tools but not in the usual fashion. I work up a rhythm and find them very relaxing to knit; the end result always justifies the work! This design uses parallel columns of twisted stitches that cross and appear to interweave at the junction points because of the direction the stitches are twisted. I especially enjoy these patterns because they were some of the first handknit ones I brought to my machine years ago. I find that the longer I have been knitting, the less I differentiate between hand and machine knitting. After all, stitches are stitches and rows are rows whether you create them on a pair of sticks or a bed of metal hooks!

YARNS
#1646 Country Pink
1 ball

NEEDLE
Size 7 (4½ mm) *or size to obtain gauge*
Two size 7 (4½ mm) double-pointed needles (dpn)

MACHINE
Mid-gauge machine
Sample knit on the Studio by White SK860

GAUGE
20 sts and 26 rows to 4" (10cm) in St st

SQUARE
Handknit version
Cast on 60 sts. Work 3 ridges, end with a WS row. Keeping first and last 3 sts in garter st, work center 54 sts in Chart pat as foll: Work rows 1–34 once, then rep rows 3–33 once more. Work 3 ridges. Bind off.

Machine-knit version

Machine knitting abbreviations
CO Cast on
COR (L) Carriage on right (left)
2RT Remove 2 sts on 2-prong transfer tool. Insert a 2nd transfer tool from back to front through the same sts, then remove the first tool. Rotate the tool one half turn to the left to return the sts to needles.
2LT Work as for 2RT, but rotate the tool one half turn to the right to return the sts to needles.

Work as for handknit version with these notes for machine knitting: Beg with COR and do latch tool CO from left to right. Use garter bar to turn work over after each of the next 6 rows is knitted, ending COR after last turn. K 1 more row, then foll chart. Whenever COL, you should be twisting sts; whenever COR, use latch tool to reform the 3 sts at each edge as k sts to cont garter border. At end of chart, k 1 plain row, then rep garter rows using garter bar. ∩

IN OTHER WORDS

RT K 2nd st on LH needle in front of first st, then k first st; sl both sts off needle.
LT With RH needle behind LH needle, k 2nd st on LH needle through back loop, k into front of first st; sl both sts off needle.

CHART *OVER 54 STS*

Row 1 (RS) K1, *[LT] twice, k12; rep from* twice more, [RT] twice, k1. **2 and all WS rows** Purl. **3** K2, LT, *LT, k10, [RT] twice; rep from* twice more, k2. **5** K3, *[LT] twice, k8, [RT] twice; rep from* twice more, k3. **7** K4, *[LT] twice, k6, [RT] twice, k2; rep from* twice more, k2. **9** K5, *[LT] twice, k4, [RT] twice, k4; rep from* twice more, k1. **11** K6, *[LT] twice, k2, [RT] twice, k6; rep from* twice more. **13** K7, *[LT] twice, [RT] twice, k8; rep from* twice more, end last rep k7. **15** K8, *LT, [RT] twice, k10; rep from* twice more, end last rep k8. **17** K9, *[LT] twice, k12; rep from* twice more, end last rep k9. **19** K8, *[RT] twice, LT, k10; rep from* twice more, end last rep k8. **21** K7, *[RT] twice, [LT] twice, k8; rep from* twice more, end last rep k7. **23** K6, *[RT] twice, k2, [LT] twice, k6; rep from* twice more. **25** K5, *[RT] twice, k4, [LT] twice, k4; rep from* twice more, k1. **27** K4, *[RT] twice, k6, [LT] twice, k2; rep from* twice more, k2. **29** K3, *[RT] twice, k8, [LT] twice; rep from* twice more, k3. **31** K2, *[RT] twice, k10, LT; rep from* twice more, LT, k2. **33** K1, [RT] twice, *k12, [LT] twice; rep from* twice more, k1. **34** Purl. Rep rows 3–33 once more.

Chart

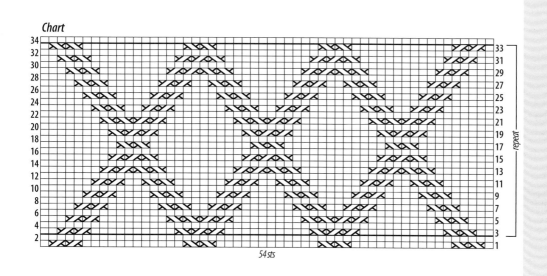

54 sts

Stitch Key
☐ K on RS, p on WS
⧖ RT
⧗ LT

Elise Duvekot
HOCKESSIN, DELAWARE

Knitting has always been part of my life. My mother grew up in the Netherlands knitting socks and sweaters for her brothers and father and, after immigrating to America, she taught me how to knit at an early age. Since times have changed, I have been fortunate enough to be able to immerse myself into the world of knitting exclusively from the vantage point of a leisure activity rather than as a utilitarian duty, and have taken to it with enthusiasm.

A native of New York, I recently returned to the United States after fifteen years of teaching, translating, and interpreting at the University of Heidelberg, Germany. One of the charms of that country is that there are spectacular yarn shops on almost every corner. Be it on a train or in a streetcar or even in the hallowed halls of learning, one can hear the clicking and clacking of needles in the hands of avid knitters (both male and female). It was in Germany that I refined my knitting, selling knitwear in boutiques in Heidelberg.

Here in the United States, my designs have been exhibited in galleries and museum shops; I have taught classes locally and at Stitches, and have designed sweaters (usually knit from the top down) for a number of publications.

In addition to the strands of yarn I knit together into patterns, I also weave words together in various languages within the scope of the translating and interpreting business I run together with my husband. I find that both knitting and translating provide ideal environments in which to be creative and productive. In this manner, it seems that I have gained access to the best of both worlds.

As far as the style of my work is concerned, it can be described as traditional in workmanship, while modern in color and design. Inspiration comes from the juxtaposition of the many beautiful colors and special yarns that have become available in recent years. Geometric designs tend to catch my eye wherever I go. My afghan square, titled "Fearless Symmetry," is certainly a reflection of that, since it is not merely symmetrical in terms of left and right, but rather it is the same on all four sides.

YARNS
MC #1602 Aran
   1 ball
A #1645 Pale
   Country Pink
   ½ ball
B #1631 Taupe
   ½ ball
C #1646 Country
   Pink
   ½ ball
D #1632 Rich Taupe
   ½ ball
E #1647 Burgandy
   ½ ball

NEEDLES
Size 7 (4½ mm) circular, 16" (40cm) long
or size to obtain gauge
Five size 7 (4½mm) double-pointed needles (dpn)

GAUGE
19 sts and 28 rows to 4" (10cm) in Chart pat

Notes
1 See *School*, p. 52 for S2KP2.
2 Change to dpn when necessary.

Square
With circular needle and MC, cast on 224 sts. Join and work in rnds as foll: *Rnd 1* *Work rnd 1 of chart over 56 sts; rep from* 3 times more. Cont in pat through chart rnd 43—8 sts. Cut yarn, leaving a 6" tail. Draw tail through rem sts and pull tog tightly. Fasten off. ∩

IN OTHER WORDS
S2KP2 Sl last 2 sts of rep tog knitwise, k first st of next rep, p2sso.

Chart *BEG ON 224 STS*
Rnd 1 With MC, *p55, k1; rep from* 3 times more. *2* K1, *k53, S2KP2; rep from* 3 times more. *3* *P53, k1; rep from* 3 times more. *4* K1, *k51, S2KP2; rep from* 3 times more. *5* *P51, k1; rep from* 3 times more. *6* K1, *k49, S2KP2; rep from* 3 times more—200 sts. *7* Knit. *8* With A, *[k4, sl 1] 9 times, k5; rep from* 3 times more. *9* K1, *k3, sl 1, [k4, sl 1] 8 times, k3, S2KP2; rep from* 3 times more. *10* K1, *k2, sl 1, [k4, sl 1] 8 times, k2, S2KP2; rep from* 3 times more—184 sts. *11* With MC, knit. *12* K1, *k43, S2KP2; rep from* 3 times more. *13* K1, *k41, S2KP2; rep from* 3 times more—168 sts. *14* Knit. *15* K1, *k39, S2KP2; rep from* 3 times more. *16* K1, *k37, S2KP2;

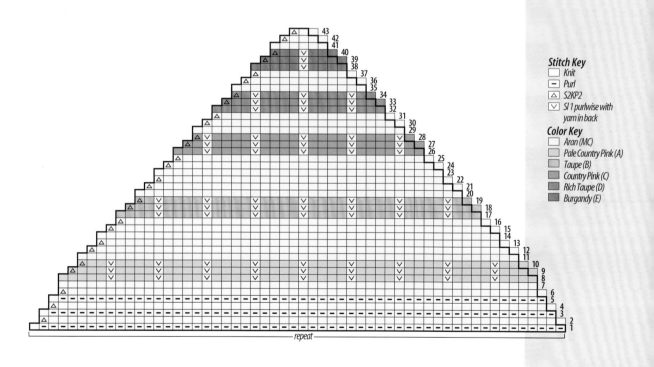

rep from* 3 times more. **17** With
B, *k3, sl 1, [k4, sl 1] 6 times, k4; rep
from* 3 times more. **18** K1, *k2, sl 1,
[k4, sl 1] 6 times, k2, S2KP2; rep from*
3 times more. **19** K1, *k1, sl 1, [k4, sl 1]
6 times, k1, S2KP2; rep from* 3 times
more—136 sts. **20** With MC, knit. **21** K1,
k31, S2KP2; rep from 3 times more.
22 K1, *k29, S2KP2; rep from* 3 times
more—120 sts. **23** Knit. **24** K1, *k27, S2KP2;
rep from* 3 times more. **25** K1, *k25, S2KP2;
rep from* 3 times more. **26** With C, *k2, sl 1,
[k4, sl 1] 4 times, k3; rep from* 3 times more.
27 K1, *k1, sl 1, [k4, sl 1] 4 times, k1, S2KP2; rep from* 3 times more. **28** K1, *sl
1, [k4, sl 1] 4 times, S2KP2; rep from* 3 times more—88 sts. **29** With MC, knit.
30 K1, *k19, S2KP2; rep from* 3 times more. **31** K1, *k17, S2KP2; rep from* 3 times
more. **32** With D, *k3, sl 1, [k4, sl 1] twice, k4; rep from* 3 times more. **33** K1,
k2, sl 1, [k4, sl 1] twice, k2, S2KP2; rep from 3 times more. **34** K1, *k1, sl 1, [k4,
sl 1] twice, k1, S2KP2; rep from* 3 times more—56 sts. **35** With MC, knit. **36** K1,
k11, S2KP2; rep from 3 times more. **37** K1, *k9, S2KP2; rep from* 3 times more.
38 With E, *k4, sl 1, k5; rep from* 3 times more. **39** K1, *k3, sl 1, k3, S2KP2; rep
from* 3 times more. **40** K1, *k2, sl 1, k2, S2KP2; rep from* 3 times more—24 sts.
41 With MC, knit. **42** K1, *k3, S2KP2; rep from* 3 times more. **43** K1, *k1, S2KP2; rep
from* 3 times more—8 sts.

Stitch Key
☐ Knit
▬ Purl
△ S2KP2
☑ Sl 1 purlwise with
   yarn in back

Color Key
☐ Aran (MC)
☐ Pale Country Pink (A)
☐ Taupe (B)
☐ Country Pink (C)
☐ Rich Taupe (D)
☐ Burgundy (E)

repeat

33

Gloria Tracy
SANTA BARBARA, CALIFORNIA

Even though I started knitting as a young adult, it quickly replaced sewing as my craft of choice. My first sweater was a cable cardigan with slanted front pockets made in red Columbia Minerva yarn. The four-year-old child it was intended for finally was able to wear it several years later. Knitting became my passionate avocation until 1991 when I quit my "day job" to work as a freelance knit and crochet designer. It has since that time been my passionate vocation.

In 1996, Susan Levin and I formed K1C2 Solutions! which markets knit and crochet kits, patterns, and unique accessories. I'm also active in design and education for the yarn industry and am a widely published writer and designer as well as an accredited professional teacher. I'm actively involved in the Professional Knitwear Designer's Guild, the Knitting Guild of America, The Crochet Guild of America, The British Knitting and Crochet Guild and manufacturing organizations such as The National Needlework Association and the Hobby Industries Association.

My square looks like a present and that's exactly what it is. Open up the pattern and you find—surprise!—the complex-looking finished square is really just unusual applications of a simple slip stitch pattern and an easy seaming technique. I've chosen the Thorn Flowers pattern because it is simple—only a four-row repeat with a four-row offset—and because it shows so clearly how you can easily get dramatic results just by reversing colors. An ordinary finishing technique, three-needle bind-off, becomes a design feature simply by placing the seam on the outside and working it in a contrasting color. Enlarged, the square would make a great pillow top. A bonus gift is the simplified way of working the ssk's. It was taught to me by Hélène Rush who learned it from her French Canadian mother. Happy (fill in the blank) everyone!

Note See *School*, p. 52 for 3-needle bind-off.
Simplified ssk Insert RH needle into front of first st, then into back of 2nd st; k these 2 sts tog.
Pat St *MULTIPLE OF 4 STS, PLUS 1*
Row 1 (RS) With MC, k2, *(k1, yo, k1) in next st, k3; rep from*, end last rep k2. *2* With CC, p2, *sl 3 with yarn in front (wyif), p3; rep from*, end last rep p2. *3* With CC, k1, *k2tog, sl 1 with yarn in back (wyib), ssk, k1; rep from* to end. *4* With MC, p4, *sl 1 wyif, p3; rep from*, end last rep p4. *5* With MC, k4, *(k1, yo, k1) in next st, k3; rep from*, end last rep k4. *6* With CC, p4, *sl 3 wyif, p3; rep from*, end last rep p4. *7* With CC, k3, *k2tog, sl 1 wyib, ssk, k1; rep from*, end last rep k3. *8* With MC, p2, *sl 1 wyif, p3; rep from*, end last rep p2. Rep rows 1–8 for Pat st.

For each square, cast on 21 sts with waste yarn, using crochet cast-on. P 1 row with C. Work rows 1–8 of Pat st 4 times, then work rows 1–4 once more. K 1 row with C. Place all sts on hold.
Squares 1 and 3 MC=B; CC= A .
Squares 2 and 4 MC=A; CC= B .
Finishing
Transfer 21 sts of Square 1 on holder to needle. Transfer cast-on sts of Square 2 to needle as foll: Pick up the purl bumps of the first row of working yarn with a smaller gauge needle (removing waste yarn), then transfer sts to separate needle. Be careful to pick up both end sts—21 sts. With RS facing and C, and using 3-needle bind-off, join top edge of Square 1 with lower edge of Square 2. In same way, join top edge of Square 4 with lower edge of Square 3. With RS facing and C, pick up and k21 sts evenly along inside edge of Square 1, pick up and k1 st in bind-off ridge, then 21 sts along inside edge of Square 2—43 sts. Repeat for inside edges of Squares 3 and 4. Join all squares using 3-needle bind-off.

YARNS
A #1602 Aran
    ½ ball
B #1647 Burgandy
    ½ ball
C #1632 Rich Taupe
    ½ ball

NEEDLES
Size 8 (5mm) needles
or size to obtain gauge
Size 8 (5mm) circular
needle, 24" (60cm)
long

EXTRAS
Crochet hook
Waste yarn
St holders & markers

GAUGE
18 sts and 29 rows to
4" (10cm) in St st

Border

With RS facing, circular needle and C, beg at upper right corner of Square 3, *k across sts on holder, pick up and k 1 st in bind-off ridge, k across sts on holder, place marker (pm) in corner, pick up and k 43 sts along next edge, pm.* Rep between *'s once—172 sts. Join, and p 1 rnd. **Next rnd** Knit, inc 1 st each side of each marker—180 sts. P 1 rnd. Rep last 2 rnds twice more, binding off 196 sts purlwise on last rnd. With 3 strands of C held tog, tie a bow and attach to center of square. ∩

CROCHET CAST-ON

1 Leaving short tail, make slip knot on crochet hook. Hold crochet hook in right hand and knitting needle on top of yarn in left hand. With hook to right of yarn, bring yarn through loop on hook; yarn goes over top of needle forming a stitch.

2 *Bring yarn under point of needle and hook yarn through loop forming next stitch; repeat from* to last stitch. Slip loop from hook to needle for last stitch.

Square 2	Square 3
Square 1	Square 4

← 4½" → 5"

Lois Young
HOUGHTON, MICHIGAN

I learned to knit when I was ten years old. No one told me that I should knit right-handed, so I sat opposite a friend and learned how to do it left-handed. She never taught me to purl, so all I could do was garter stitch, which I didn't consider "knitting." In college, someone said that purling was the opposite of knitting. It took me quite a while to figure out how those words fit the action of purling, but I did it, and have been knitting ever since. My first sweater was a yoke sweater with bands of lace, which must have been prophetic, because I wrote a column on lace knitting for a number of years and now designing yoke sweaters is my current design interest.

My first design was made out of desperation. My parents brought me some gorgeous mohair from Canada and there wasn't enough of it to finish any pattern I found, so I made up my own. Later I was fortunate to discover Elizabeth Zimmermann's first book. I think I memorized the book and soon began experimenting on my own. I'm one of the two charter members (who have attended every year) of Elizabeth and Meg's knitting camp. I love the encouragement, good ideas, and thought exchanges between kindred spirits.

In my other life, I teach calculus at an engineering university, garden, grow orchids, read mysteries, spoil my three cats, and enjoy my family.

Having to translate my left-handed knitting to fit into a right-handed world has helped me visualize stitch patterns and processes. My square uses texture to show a blossoming vine. I like curves and flowers, so this vine is a good way to incorporate both. The vines look like traveling stitch, but in fact are a paired increase and decrease. I find that the stems lie flatter with this method of traveling, and the traveling stitch doesn't get elongated the way it sometimes does with a more conventional approach. The chart is written for right-handed knitters, but it can be worked left-handed if the ssk is worked as a k2tog and vice versa.

YARNS
MC #1645 Pale
   Country Pink
   ½ ball

NEEDLES
Size 7 (4½ mm) *or size to obtain gauge*

GAUGE
19 sts and 27 rows to 4" (10cm) over Chart pat (after blocking)

Note
See *School*, p.52 for M1 purl left-slanting (M1L), M1 purl right-slanting (M1R), and ssk.
Square
Cast on 57 sts. Work 3 ridges, end with a RS row. Keeping first and last 3 sts in garter st, work center 51 sts in Chart pat as foll:
Row 1 (WS) Reading chart from left to right, work 12-st rep of chart 4 times, then work last 3 sts of chart. Cont in pat as established through chart row 71. Work 3 ridges. Bind off. ⌒

IN OTHER WORDS
CHART *OVER 51 STS*
Row 1 (WS) [K5, p1, k6] 4 times, k3. *2* P3, [p5, k2tog, M1L, p5] 4 times. *3* [K6, p1, k5] 4 times, k3. *4* P3, [p4, k2tog, M1L, p6] 4 times. *5* [K7, p1, k4] 4 times, k3. *6* P3, [p3, k2tog, M1L, p7] 4 times. *7* [K8, p1, k3] 4 times, k3. *8* P3, [p2, k2, p8] 4 times. *9* [K8, p3, k1] 4 times, k3. *10* P3, [k3, M1R, ssk, p7] 4 times. *11* [K7, p1, k1, p3] 4 times, k3. *12* P3, [k3, p1, M1R, ssk, p6] 4 times. *13* [K6, p1, k2, p3] 4 times, k3. *14* P3, [k2, p3, M1R, ssk, p5] 4 times. *15* [K5, p1] 8 times, k3. *16* P3, [p6, k1, p5] 4 times. *17* [K5, p1, k6] 4 times, k3. *18* P3, [p5, k2tog, M1L, p5] 4 times. *19* [K6, p1, k5] 4 times, k3. *20* P3, [p4, k2tog, M1L, k1, p5] 4 times. *21* [K5, p1, k1, p1, k4] 4 times, k3. *22* P3, [p3, k2tog, M1L, k3, p4] 4 times. *23* [K4, p3, k1, p1, k3] 4 times, k3. *24* P3, [p2, k2tog, M1L, k5, p3] 4 times. *25 and 27* [K3, p5, k1, p1, k2] 4 times, k3. *26* P3, [p2, k1, p1, k5, p3] 4 times. *28* P3, [p2, (k1, p1) 4 times, p2] 4 times. *29* [K3, (p1, k1) 4 times, k1] 4 times, k3. *30* P3, [p2, k1, p3, k1, p5] 4 times. *31* [K9, p1, k2] 4 times, k3. *32* P3, [p2, M1R, ssk, p8] 4 times. *33* [K8, p1, k3] 4 times, k3. *34* P3, [p3, M1R, ssk, p7] 4 times. *35* [K7, p1, k4] 4 times, k3. *36* P3, [p4, M1R, ssk, p6]

4 times. **37** [K6, p1, k5] 4 times, k3. **38** P3,
[p5, k2, p5] 4 times. **39** [K4, p3, k5] 4
times, k3. **40** P3, [p4, k2tog, M1L, k3,
p3] 4 times. **41** [K3, p3, k1, p1, k4] 4
times, k3. **42** P3, [p3, k2tog, M1L,
p1, k3, p3] 4 times. **43** [K3, p3,
k2, p1, k3] 4 times, k3. **44** P3, [p2,
k2tog, M1L, p3, k2, p3] 4 times. **45** [K3, p1, k5,
p1, k2] 4 times, k3. **46** P3, [p2, k1, p9] 4 times. **47** [K9, p1, k2] 4 times,
k3. **48** P3, [p2, M1R, ssk, p8] 4 times. **49** [K8, p1, k3] 4 times, k3. **50** P3, [p2, k1,
M1R, ssk, p7] 4 times. **51** [K7, p1, k1, p1, k2] 4 times, k3. **52** P3, [p1, k3, M1R, ssk,
p6] 4 times. **53** [K6, p1, k1, p3, k1] 4 times, k3. **54** P3, [k5, M1R, ssk, p5] 4 times.
55 and 57 [K5, p1, k1, p5] 4 times, k3. **56** P3, [k5, p1, k1, p5] 4 times. **58** P3, [(k1, p1) 4
times, p4] 4 times. **59** [K5, (p1, k1) 3 times, p1] 4 times, k3. **60** P3, [p2, k1, p2, k2tog,
M1L, p5] 4 times. **61** [K6, p1, k5] 4 times, k3. **62** P3, [p4, k2tog, M1L, p6] 4 times.
63 [K7, p1, k4] 4 times, k3. **64** P3, [p2, k1, k2tog, M1L, p7] 4 times. **65** [K8, p3, k1] 4
times, k3. **66** P3, [k4, p8] 4 times. **67** [K9, p3] 4 times, k3. **68** P3, [k2, p10] 4 times.
69 [K11, p1] 4 times, k3. **70** Purl. **71** Knit.

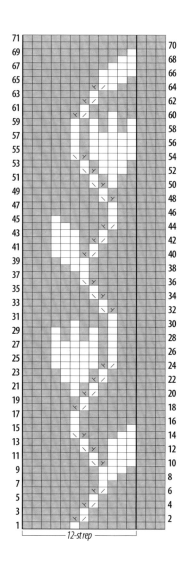

Stitch Key
☐ *Knit on RS*
▨ *Knit on WS*
◿ *K2tog*
◺ *Ssk*
⊠ *M1L*
⊠ *M1R*

37

Sue Flanders
ROBBINSDALE, MINNESOTA

I imagine that it has something to do with being from "minne-snow-ta", but I feel that the strongest influence in my knitting designs is from Norwegian knitting. At 12 years old, I remember being in awe when my older sister knit a forest green Norwegian sweater with white snowflakes and moose. It wasn't until I was a freshman in college, during January term, that I actually knit my first Norwegian sweater. I would stay up half the night knitting—I couldn't wait to see how it was going to turn out.

This square has a unique feature in that it uses two-color knitting in the round, a very Norwegian technique, and still remains square. The decreases at the corners became part of the snowflake pattern which makes a very attractive design element. Traditional Norwegian sweaters have a main color, a contrasting color and a "touch of color" which is reflected in the color choices in the square.

I have designed a large number of fun, funky hats and children's sweaters for Three Kittens Designs. I have also been published in Knitter's and Better Homes & Gardens Country Craft magazines. I was absolutely thrilled to be included in Knitting in America by Melanie Fallick. Also I have recently completed a project that will be included in Melanie's new Kids Knitting book.

Currently the challenge for me is to find time to knit and explore design options. I work full time as an Industrial Hygienist for the State of Minnesota and spend most of my free time with my husband and five-year-old daughter. Because of the time crunch, I find myself gravitating to smaller, more manageable-sized projects. I have also had to cut down the number of knitting-related yearly trips to Stitches and other such conventions.

YARNS
A #1602 Aran
   ½ ball
B #1647 Burgandy
   ½ ball
C #1645 Pale
   Country Pink
   ½ ball

NEEDLES
Size 7 (4½mm)
circular needle,
24" (60cm) long *or
size to obtain gauge*
Size 7 (4½mm)
double-pointed
needles (dpn)

EXTRAS
Tapestry needle
Four split stitch
markers

GAUGE
19 sts and 20 rows to
4" (10cm) in St st

Notes
1 See *School*, p.52 for S2KP2.
2 End all rnds 1 st before beg of foll rnd.
3 Chart pat does not include 2 sl sts of dec (k st of dec is first st of chart).
4 Change to dpn when necessary.

Square
With circular needle and A, cast on 224 sts. Join, being careful not to twist sts. **Rnd 1** P to 1 st before end of rnd (see Note 2 above), placing marker in 1st, 57th, 113th and 169th sts to mark corners. **2** Attach B, *S2KP2, k to 1 st before next marker; rep from* around. **3** With B, purl. **4** With A, *S2KP2, k to 1 st before next marker; rep from* around. **5** With A, purl. **Beg Chart pat: Rnd 1** With C, *sl 2 sts tog knitwise, k first st of chart, p2sso, k to last st of chart; rep from* around. Cont in pat through chart rnd 25, working dec at corner every rnd—8 sts. Fasten off. Draw yarn through sts and pull tog tightly.

Finishing
Block square. With tapestry needle and C, work French knots in center of square as shown. ∩

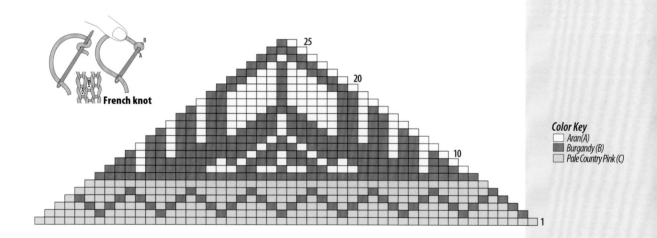

French knot

25

20

10

1

Linda Cyr
CINCINNATI, OHIO

For my first 28 years, I was a repressed creative person. I graduated from Princeton with a degree in engineering and worked in marketing and management for a large company, but my real career goal was to be a knitting designer.

When my second child was born, I jumped off the corporate ladder and became a full-time mother. After both kids were sleeping through the night, I decided that it was "now or never" and started my design career. I have spent my days being mom, wife, housekeeper, cook, chauffeur, but at night, I fire up the computer and the knitting needles. The past few years have been a blur of knitting and sleep deprivation, but my design work gives me a sense of accomplishment that I will never find elsewhere. I've also met some great people from the knitting universe who I now regard as friends.

To keep life interesting, I had my third child last year and moved into a century-old house that we are renovating. I've put my knit designing on hold, but I'm sure that won't last. Whenever baby and schedule permit, I pick up my knitting. It satisfies me on so many levels and is a part of who I am; but even cashmere cannot compete with the softness of my little one's cheeks!

My square is an adaptation of a traditional quilt block called "monkey wrench." I confess to being a garter stitch snob—I've never liked it much, but after spending time tinkering around with it for Knitter's K47 (focus on simple stitches), I developed a new appreciation for this easiest of stitch patterns. I enjoyed working this square because once the numbers are figured out, it is pretty much mindless knitting and as the knitting spirals out from the center, there are very few ends to weave in when you are finished. (Editors update: In September '99 Linda had her fourth child.)

YARNS
A #1602 Aran
   1 ball
B #1646 Country
   Pink
   ½ ball

NEEDLES
Size 7 (4½ mm) *or size to obtain gauge*

GAUGE
20 sts and 40 rows to 4" (10cm) in garter st (k every row)

Notes
1 Foll diagram for placement of squares and triangles and color of triangles.
2 For ease in working, mark RS of Square 1.
SK2P Sl 1 st knitwise, k2tog, pass the sl st over.

Square 1
With A, cast on 6 sts. K 10 rows. **Next row** (RS) Bind off, do not cut yarn; place loop on hold.

Square 2
With RS facing and B, pick up and k6 sts along right side of Square 1. K 9 rows. Bind off as for Square 1.

Square 3
With RS facing and separate ball of A, pick up and k6 sts along right side of Square 2. Complete as for Square 2.

Square 4
With separate ball of B, pick up and k6 sts along right side of Square 3. Complete as for Square 2.

Triangle 5
Place last bound-off loop from Square 4 on needle and with RS facing, pick up and k10 more sts along Squares 4 and 3—11 sts. Work in garter st and dec 1 st each side every RS row until 3 sts rem. **Next row** SK2P. Do not cut yarn. Place st on hold.

Triangles 6, 7, and 8
Using last bound-off loop from Squares 3, 2 and 1, work as for Triangle 5.

Triangles 9, 10, 11, and 12
Work as before, picking up 14 sts in addition to bound-off loop.

Triangles 13, 14, 15, and 16
Work as before, picking up 20 sts in addition to bound-off loop.

Triangles 17, 18, 19, and 20
Work as before, picking up 28 sts in addition to bound-off loop.

Triangles 21, 22, 23, and 24
Work as before, picking up 40 sts in addition to bound-off loop.

Finishing
Fasten off all loops. Sew seam to join Squares 1 and 4. ∩

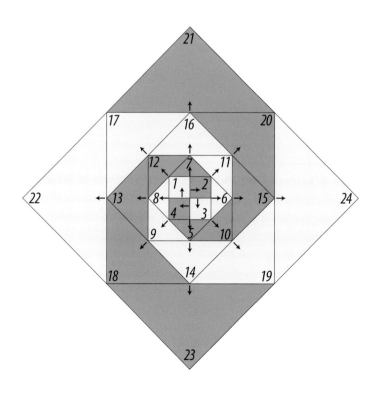

Color Key
☐ Aran (A)
▨ Country Pink (B)
↑ Direction of knitting

Shirley Paden
NEW YORK, NEW YORK

I learned to knit when I was nine during a summer visit to my grandmother. I sat beside her every afternoon, looking up from my reading, mesmerized by the beautiful, lacy piece growing from her needles as she rocked back and forth. With her fingers seemingly dancing in the air, she made the construction of the lace shawl seem effortless. She was an expert knitter and crochet artist, often working on commissioned pieces. When she determined that my interest was genuine and that I had a long enough attention span, she handed me two needles and a ball of yarn.

For a number of years my needlework interest never waned. I knit and crocheted hats, scarves, and shawls during high school and college. However, my knitting repertoire was severely restricted as I only knew garter, stockinette, and k1, p1 ribbing. I could not read patterns and knew no colorwork techniques.

After college I put away my needlework and became completely involved in my corporate career path. I did not touch a knitting needle or crochet hook for 16 years. Eight years ago someone in my office was working on her first knitting project and asked me if I knew how to bind off. As I took the project into my hands, suddenly a switch was turned on. I visited a yarn shop across from my office that very afternoon. During the next 12 months, I averaged a project every two weeks. The yarn shop encouraged me to learn new techniques and they coached me through difficult projects such as Kaffe Fassett's "Midnight Carnation."

The following year I left the corporate world, traded my briefcase for a knitting bag, and launched Shirley Paden Custom Knits. I began by designing a Christmas collection with 12 evening sweaters. Today, I continue to design. I also teach advanced techniques, design, and finishing in the Continuing Education Department of Parsons School of Design and The New School for Social Research as well as various local workshops.

This swatch represents the knitting technique that was my first love—colorwork. It also represents spring which for me is always a time of joy. When you knit the entire afghan, it is my hope that your eyes will scan the beautiful squares and as you see this one your heart will be warmed with thoughts of sunshine and bloom!

YARNS
#1602 Aran
1 ball
#1632 Rich Taupe
½ ball
#1646 Country Pink
½ ball
#1645 Pale Country Pink
½ ball

NEEDLES
Size 7 (4½mm) *or size to obtain gauge*

GAUGE
20 sts and 27 rows to 4" (10cm) in St st

Square
With ecru, cast on 61 sts. Work 3 ridges, end with a WS row. Keeping first and last 3 sts in garter st with ecru, work center 55 sts in Chart pat for 5 rows. **Beg Short rows: *Next row** (WS) K3, wrap next p st, turn, k3, turn, work in pat across all sts, hiding p wrap. **Next row** (RS) K3, wrap next k st, turn, k3, turn, work in pat across all sts, hiding k wrap. Work 2 rows even. Rep from* through chart row 70, ending last rep work 3 rows even. Work 3 ridges with ecru. Bind off. ∩

SHORT ROW WRAP, KNIT SIDE

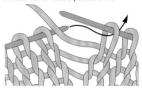

With yarn in back, slip next stitch as if to purl. Bring yarn to front of work and slip stitch back to left needle as shown. Turn work

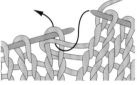

When you come to the wrap on a right-side row, make it less visible by working the wrap together with the stitch it wraps.

PURL SIDE

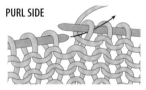

With yarn in front, slip next stitch as if to purl. Bring yarn to back of work and slip stitch back to left needle as shown. Turn work.

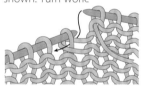

When you come to the wrap on the following purl row, make it less visible by inserting right needle under wrap as shown, placing the wrap on the left needle, and purling it together with the stitch it wraps.

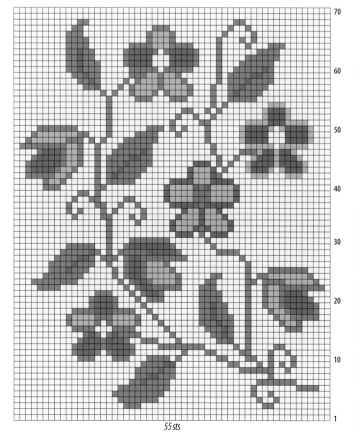

55 sts

Color Key
☐ Aran
▨ Rich Taupe
▨ Country Pink
▨ Pale Country Pink

Gayle Bunn
TORONTO, ONTARIO

My grandmother taught me to knit when I was about 6. I was immediately in love with the combinations of texture, color, and the tactile experience of working with yarn. From that day on I've thought of knitting as a fun learning journey, which I'm still on after all these years.

I studied fashion design at Ryerson College in Toronto and always included handknit designs among my projects. After graduating and then traveling around Europe, I returned to Toronto and sold sweaters to local shops. I then began to consider a serious career in knitwear design. I took a chance and wrote a letter of introduction to Patons—the most recognized yarn company in Canada. Fate was on my side as two of their senior designers had just retired and they were looking for a new designer with fresh ideas. I started as a pattern writer/designer with the company in August 1986.

Today I'm the Design Manager for Patons where I oversee the production of our pattern publications. It's a fun and challenging career, which I love. I have a wonderful family—my husband Stephen (a landscape designer), my son Keith (who proudly wears his Mom's creations), and a new baby born in May '99.

This afghan square combines my favorite knitting techniques with inspiration from vintage knitwear styling. Cables and Fair Isle are mediums in which I love to design and knit. The rose is in honor of the many gardens from my past (my father is also a landscape designer) and my present with Stephen. I worked the rose in duplicate stitch, which is a technique very similar to needlepoint, that is another of my favorite crafts.

YARNS
MC #1602 Aran
    1 ball
A   #1631 Taupe
    small amount
B   #1646 Country
    Pink
    small amount
C   #1645 Pale
    Country Pink
    small amount
D   #1647 Burgandy
    small amount
E   #1636 Sage Green
    small amount

NEEDLES
Size 7 (4½ mm) *or size to obtain gauge*

EXTRAS
Cable needle (cn)

GAUGE
20 sts and 26 rows to 4" (10cm) in St st (k on RS, p on WS)

Notes
1 See *School*, p. 52 for M1 knit, M1 purl, and duplicate st.
2 Square is made in sections: cable strips, center square, and side borders for center square.

Square
Cable strip *MAKE 4*
With MC, cast on 2 sts. **Work Chart A** Work chart rows 1–19, [work rows 12–19] 7 times, work rows 20-35 (91 rows). Fasten off last st.

Center square
With A, cast on 37 sts. K 1 row. P 1 row. **Beg Chart B: Row 1** (RS) [Work chart sts 1–8] 4 times, work sts 1–5. Work through chart row 3. With A, p 2 rows, dec 2 sts on 2nd row—35 sts. With MC, work 41 rows in St st. With A, k 3 rows, inc 2 sts on first row—37 sts. **Beg Chart B: Row 1** (WS) Reading chart from left to right, work chart sts 5–1, [work sts 8–1] 4 times. Work through chart row 3. With A, work 2 rows in St st. Bind off all sts.

Side borders
With RS facing and A, pick up and k45 sts evenly along side of center square. K 2 rows. **Beg Chart B: Row 1** (WS) [Work chart sts 9–2] 5 times, work sts 9–5. Work through chart row 3. With A, work 2 rows in St st. Bind off all sts. Rep for other side.

Finishing
Work Chart C in duplicate st over MC portion of center square. Sew cable strips to sides of square. Sew mitred corners.

Eyelet border
With RS facing and MC, pick up and k55 sts evenly along one side of square. **Row 1** (WS) Knit. **2** K1, *yo, k2tog; rep from* to end. **3 and 4** Knit. Bind off knitwise on WS. Rep for opposite side. With RS facing, pick up and k59 sts evenly across top of square, including side borders. Work 4-row eyelet border. Rep for lower edge. ∩

IN OTHER WORDS

3/3 RC Sl 3 to cn, hold to back, k3; k3 from cn.
3/3 LC Sl 3 to cn, hold to front, k3; k3 from cn.

CHART A *2 STS, INC'D TO 11 STS, DEC'D TO 1 ST*
Row 1 (WS) K2. **2** K1, M1 knit (M1K), k1. **3** K1, M1 purl (M1P), p1, k1. **4** K3, M1K, k1. **5** K1, M1P, p3, k1. **6** K5, M1K, k1. **7** K1, M1P, p5, k1. **8** K7, M1K, k1. **9** K1, M1P, p7, k1. **10** K1, 3/3 RC, k2, M1K, k1. **11, 13, 15, 17, 19** K1, p9, k1. **12, 16** Knit. **14** K4, 3/3 LC, k1. **18** K1, 3/3 RC, k4. **20, 24** Knit. **21, 23, 25** K1, p9, k1. **22** K4, 3/3 LC, k1. **26** K1, 3/3 RC, k1, k2tog, k1. **27** K1, p2tog, p6, k1. **28** K6, k2tog, k1. **29** K1, p2tog, p4, k1. **30** K4, k2tog, k1. **31** K1, p2tog, p2, k1. **32** K2, k2tog, k1. **33** K1, p2tog, k1. **34** K1, k2tog. **35** P2tog.

Chart A

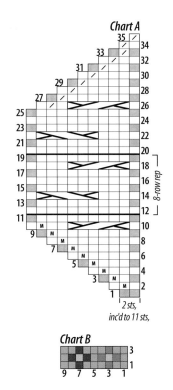

2 sts,
inc'd to 11 sts,

Chart B

9 7 5 3 1

Chart C

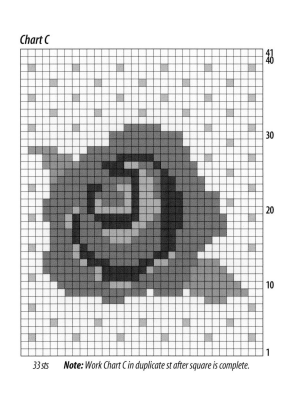

33 sts   **Note:** *Work Chart C in duplicate st after square is complete.*

Stitch Key
- ☐ K on RS, p on WS
- ▨ P on RS, k on WS
- Ⓜ M1K on RS, M1P on WS
- ╱ K2tog on RS, p2tog on WS
- ⤬ 3/3 RC
- ⤬ 3/3 LC

Color Key
- ☐ Aran (MC)
- ▨ Taupe (A)
- ▨ Country Pink (B)
- ▨ Pale Country Pink (C)
- ▨ Burgandy (D)
- ▨ Sage Green (E)

Anna Zilboorg
MEADOWS OF DAN, VIRGINIA

As an Anglican solitary, my major work is prayer; knitting is secondary. So when I came to make this square my thoughts turned to a labyrinth. There is a labyrinth set in the floor of Chartres Cathedral. Medieval pilgrimages ended at its center: the symbolic New Jerusalem. A canvas replica of this labyrinth has been showing up around the country for a walking meditation. I find it a quite wonderful spiritual exercise. I wondered what it would be like to knit a labyrinth.

I took a Celtic pattern as a template and modified it so that, entering at the bottom and always proceeding in a straight line until blocked, you come at last to the serene center. (Move a finger bump by knitted bump along this path and you might experience a semblance of the walk.)

As for the knitting: it was really a lot of fun. Garter and slip stitch couldn't be simpler technically. The complexity comes from following the rows. This is easier than at first glance if, instead of counting the stitches to be knit, you simply note where they line up with previously slipped stitches of the same color, or where the stitches you are going to slip line up with previously knit stitches. If you discover that you've made a mistake, it's easy to drop a stitch down any number of ridges and pick it back up the way you want (use a crochet hook!).

Note
1 See *School*, p. 52 for for twisting yarns when working intarsia.

Mosaic chart notes
1 Each chart row consists of k sts and sl sts (or just k sts). Sts to be knit each row are indicated at the right of chart; all other sts in chart row are slipped purlwise with yarn at WS of work.
2 Each chart row is worked twice, once on RS; then on WS, knitting or slipping the same sts as on the RS row.
3 Use separate bobbin of yarn for each large block of color, as indicated in instructions.

Square
With A, cast on 55 sts. Work 3 ridges, end with a WS row. ***Beg Chart pat: Row 1*** (RS) K3A, join B and work chart row 1 over center 49 sts, join 2nd bobbin of A and k rem 3 sts. *2* K3A, with B work row 2 to last 3 sts, k3A. *3, 4* Work with same bobbin of A across entire row as foll: k3, work chart pat over 49 sts, k3. Cont in pat as established, working A rows with 1 bobbin and B rows with 3 bobbins, through chart row 36. ***Row 37*** (RS) K3A, with B, work first 17 sts of chart, join separate bobbin of A and k15, join separate bobbin of B and work to last 3 sts, k3A. Cont in pat, working A rows with 1 bobbin and B rows with 5 bobbins, through chart row 62. Cut 2 center bobbins and work as before through chart row 98. With A, work 3 ridges. Bind off. ⌒

YARNS
A   #1631 Taupe
    ½ ball
B   #1647 Burgandy
    ½ ball

NEEDLES
Size 7 (4½mm) *or size to obtain gauge*

GAUGE
18 sts and 40 rows to 4" (10cm) in Chart pat

Color Key
□ Taupe (A)
■ Burgandy (B)

49 sts

Zabeth Loisel
STATEN ISLAND, NEW YORK

It is difficult to remember precisely when I learned to knit. It seems that my French mother, who knit non-stop for the family, took time to teach me. I can recall numerous times I sat on the arm of her chair watching her fingers in motion. It always amazes me when I watch my fingers making the same movements. She always chose patterns with full-fashioned details and pointed out to me what made sweaters so special. She taught me to count rows and not to rely on a tape measure for accuracy. She never considered beginning a sweater without checking the gauge and she constantly emphasized finishing.

Although knitting has always been a part of my life, it was only when I came to the United States that it became my working life. I had been encouraged by friends, then by professionals, to submit designs for publications. As soon as I entered the field, it proved the right thing for me. I must admit that my interest in crafts in general and knitting in particular was very much on my side. After more than a decade my enthusiasm remains intact. I always carry my knitting. I never know when my fingers will want to dance and nothing is more frustrating than having the desire to knit and having no knitting to do!

It is exciting to still be learning and to realize that there is much more to explore. There are constant possibilities for knitters to share their experiences, techniques, discoveries, influences, and stimulation.

For my square I thought that I would work around from the outside to the center and include some of my old favorites (traveling and twisted stitches, embroidery in tone on tone) and that I would improvise, discovering as I went. As the square grew, I liked its flowery look. It made me think of a rose window with patterns evolving from patterns. The pinwheels, small on the sides and large at the center are my favorite types of embroidery. They look magical when complete. The pink bobbles are present to echo other squares and to give this one a sense of belonging.

YARNS
MC #1602 Aran
1 ball
CC #1646 Country
Pink
½ ball

NEEDLES
Size 6 (4mm) circular,
16" (40cm) long *or
size to obtain gauge*
Five size 6 (4mm)
double-pointed
needles (dpn)

GAUGE
20 sts and 28 rows to
4" (10cm) in St st

Note
Change to dpn when necessary.

Square
With circular needle and MC, cast on 216 sts. Join and work in rnds as foll: **Rnd 1** *Work rnd 1 of chart over 54 sts; rep from* 3 times more. Cont in pat through chart rnd 43—24 sts. Cut yarn, leaving a 6" tail. Draw tail through rem sts and pull tog. Fasten off.

Finishing
Block square. With CC, work Herringbone st on St st between rows 7–9. With MC, work larger pinwheel at center of square, with spokes beg at rnd 41. Work 8 smaller pinwheels, foll chart for placement of center, with spokes approx 5 sts long. ⌒

IN OTHER WORDS
K1 tbl K 1 st through back loop.

Make bobble (MB) K into front, back, front of a st, turn, p3, turn, k3, turn, p3, turn, k3, pass 2nd and 3rd sts over first st and off needle.

S2KP Sl last 2 sts of rep tog knitwise, k first st of next rep, p2sso.

S2PP Sl last 2 sts of rep tog purlwise, p first st of next rep, p2sso.

1/1 Twist RPC Sl 1 to cn, hold to back, k1 tbl; p1 from cn.

1/1 Twist LPC Sl 1 to cn, hold to front, p1; k1 tbl from cn.

1/2 Twist LC Sl 2 to cn, hold to front, k1 tbl; sl last st from cn to LH needle and k1 tbl; then k1 tbl from cn.

Weiner

2/1 RPC Sl 1 to cn, hold to back, k2; p1 from cn.

2/1 LPC Sl 2 to cn, hold to front, p1; k2 from cn.

2/1 Twist RC Sl 1 to cn, hold to back, k2; k1 tbl from cn.

2/1 Twist LC Sl 2 to cn, hold to front, k1 tbl; k2 from cn.

3/1 Rib RC Sl 1 to cn, hold to back, k1, p1, k1; p1 from cn.

3/1 Rib LC Sl 3 to cn, hold to front, p1; k1, p1, k1 from cn.

2/3 Twist LC Sl 3 to cn, hold to front, k2; sl last st from cn to LH needle and k1 tbl; then k2 from cn.

2/3 Twist LPC Sl 3 to cn, hold to front, k2 tbl; sl last st from cn to LH needle and p1; then k2 tbl from cn.

2/3 LPC Sl 3 to cn, hold to front, k2; sl last st from cn to LH needle and p1; then k2 from cn.

3/4 Rib LC Sl 4 to cn, hold to front, k1, p1, k1; sl last st from cn to LH needle and p1; then k1, p1, k1 from cn.

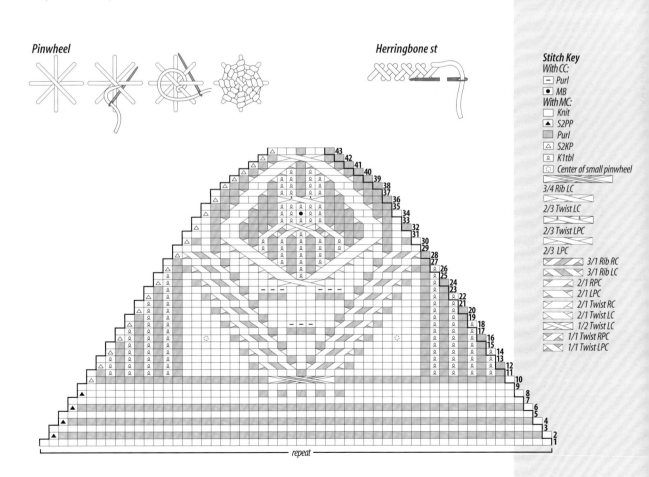

Pinwheel

Herringbone st

Stitch Key

With CC:
- ⊟ Purl
- ● MB

With MC:
- ☐ Knit
- ▲ S2PP
- ▦ Purl
- △ S2KP
- ♀ K1tbl
- ⊡ Center of small pinwheel

3/4 Rib LC

2/3 Twist LC

2/3 Twist LPC

2/3 LPC

3/1 Rib RC

3/1 Rib LC

2/1 RPC

2/1 LPC

2/1 Twist RC

2/1 Twist LC

1/2 Twist LC

1/1 Twist RPC

1/1 Twist LPC

repeat

Stephanie
MADERA, CALIFORNIA

Compared to many other contributors, I was a late starter. I learned to crochet in the late '70s as a teenager in Southern California. I studied art and design in college and didn't tackle knitting until I moved to New York City in 1981. A self-taught knitter, I knit every spare minute, but finish few pieces because I rip out and reuse the same yarn over and over. I learned a lot by trying all the pattern stitches in Vogue Knitting. That was before I discovered Knitter's and bought all the back issues.

Five years later, I had a position as assistant editor at McCall's Needlework & Crafts and in 1988 began working as a freelance designer full time. My family and I live in central California and I'm currently attending California State University Fresno. Growing up in California, I didn't know any knitters and living here today, I find more crocheters than knitters. Even those who both crochet and knit think crocheting is easier. On the East Coast, it seems to be the opposite.

The pattern in this square, which I designed ten or so years ago, is special to me. It's interesting how designs evolve. Inspiration can come from many places. This pattern has two sources of inspiration. It is a variation on traditional diamond patterns from the British Isles. My favorite patterns to knit are those which include combinations of stockinette, reverse stockinette, seed or garter stitch, and lace. The resulting fabrics are non-curling and have a nice body to them, but are also lightweight. The patterns are quick to learn and are not boring to knit because you always seem to be beginning and ending a repeat at the same time.

I was very excited at the time by the designs of the French couturier, Christian Lacroix. I love his use of color and mixture of patterns, and also his exaggerated fashion sketches, though his designs are much tamer now than in the days when he made the famous "pouf" for the house of Patou. I never knit a pouf dress (except for a Barbie doll), but a Lacroix dress design with an orange full skirt quilted in a diamond pattern and accented with pompons inspired me to create this variation of a traditional pattern.

I made myself a giant, oversized sweater using this pattern with a rolled and ribbed edge of a bulky-weight yarn similar to Reynolds' Lopi in a bright Kelly green yarn. I first used it professionally for the central pattern of an afghan in McCall's Needlework & Crafts and several years later made the sweater in off-white for Classic Elite, which later appear in their book, Knitting the New Classics.

YARNS
#1646 Country Pink
1 ball

NEEDLE
Size 7 (4½ mm) *or size to obtain gauge*
Two size 7 (4½ mm) double-pointed needles (dpn)

GAUGE
20 sts and 26 rows to 4" (10cm) in St st

Note
See *School*, p.52 for ssk.

Square
Cast on 55 sts. Work 3 ridges, end with a RS row. Keeping first and last 3 sts in garter st, work center 49 sts in Chart pat as foll: Work chart rows 1–41 once, then work rows 10-25 once more. K 3 rows. Work chart rows 1–5. Work 3 ridges. Bind off all sts. ∩

IN OTHER WORDS
Make Bobble (MB) [K1, (yo, k1) twice] in a st, turn; [sl 1, p4, turn; sl 1, k4, turn] twice; sl 1, [p2tog] twice, turn;Sl 1 knitwise, K2tog, psso.

CHART *OVER 49 STS*
Rows 1 and 5 (WS) *P2tog, yo; rep from*, end k1. *2, 3, 4, 6, 7, 8* Knit. *9* [P2tog, yo] twice, p41, [yo, p2tog] twice. *10* K4, [k1, yo, ssk, k15, k2tog, yo] twice, k5. *11* K4, [p20, k1] twice, k3. *12* K5, *k1, yo, ssk, k6, MB, k6, k2tog, yo, k1*, p1, rep from * to * once, k5. *13* [P2tog, yo] twice, p1, [k1, p8,

Gildersleeve

sl 1, p8, k1, p1] twice, [yo, p2tog] twice. **14** K4, [k1, p1, k1, yo, ssk, k11, k2tog, yo, k1, p1] twice, k5. **15** K4, p1, *p1, k1, p15, k1, p1*, k1, rep from * to * once, p1, k4. **16** K5, *k1, p1, k1, yo, ssk, k4, MB, k4, k2tog, yo, k1, p1, k1*, p1, rep from * to * once, k5. **17** [P2tog, yo] twice, [(p1, k1) twice, p6, sl 1, p6, k1, p1, k1] twice, p1, [yo, p2tog] twice. **18** K5, [(p1, k1) twice, yo, ssk, k7, k2tog, yo, (k1, p1) twice, k1] twice, k4. **19** K4, p1, *[p1, k1] twice, p11, [k1, p1] twice*, k1, rep from * to * once, p1, k4. **20** K5, *[k1, p1] twice, k1, yo, ssk, k2, MB, k2, k2tog, yo, [k1, p1] twice, k1*, p1, rep from * to * once, k5. **21** [P2tog, yo] twice, [(p1, k1) 3 times, p4, sl 1, p4, (k1, p1) twice, k1] twice, p1, [yo, p2tog] twice. **22** K4, [(k1, p1) 3 times, k1, yo, ssk, k3, k2tog, yo, (k1, p1) 3 times] twice, k5. **23** K4, p2, [k1, p1] 3 times, p6, [k1, p1] 7 times, p6, [k1, p1] 3 times, p1, k4. **24** K5, *[k1, p1] 3 times, k1, yo, ssk, k1, k2tog, yo, [k1, p1] 3 times, k1*, p1, rep from * to * once, k5. **25** [P2tog, yo] twice, [p1, k1] 4 times, p5, [k1, p1] 8 times, p4, [k1, p1] 4 times, [yo, p2tog] twice. **26** [K12, k2tog, yo, k1, yo, ssk, k3] twice, k9. **27** K4, [p10, k1, p9] twice, p1, k4. **28** K5, *k6, k2tog, yo, k1, p1, k1, yo, ssk, k6*, MB, rep from * to * once, k5. **29** [P2tog, yo] twice, p1, *p8, k1, p1, k1, p8*, sl 1, rep from * to * once, p1, [yo, p2tog] twice. **30** [K10, k2tog, yo, (k1, p1) twice, k1, yo, ssk, k1] twice, k9. **31** K4, [p8, (k1, p1) 3 times, p6] twice, p1, k4. **32** K5, *k4, k2tog, yo, [k1, p1] 3 times, k1, yo, ssk, k4*, MB, rep from * to * once, k5. **33** [P2tog, yo] twice, p1, *p6, [k1, p1] 4 times, p5*, sl 1, rep from * to * once, p1, [yo, p2tog] twice. **34** K1, [k7, k2tog, yo, (k1, p1) 4 times, k1, yo, ssk] twice, k8. **35** K4, p1, [p5, (k1, p1) 5 times, p5] twice, k4. **36** K5, *k2, k2tog, yo, [k1, p1] 5 times, k1, yo, ssk, k2*, MB, rep from * to * once, k5. **37** [P2tog, yo] twice, p1, *p4, [k1, p1] 6 times, p3*, sl 1, rep from * to * once, p1, [yo, p2tog] twice. **38** K6, *k2tog, yo, [k1, p1] 6 times, k1, yo, ssk*, k3, rep from * to * once, k6. **39** K4, [p4, (k1, p1) 7 times, p2] twice, p1, k4. **40** K5, *k2tog, yo, [k1, p1] 7 times, k1, yo, ssk*, k1, rep from * to * once, k5. **41** [P2tog, yo] twice, [p3, (k1, p1) 8 times, p1] twice, p1, [yo, p2tog] twice.

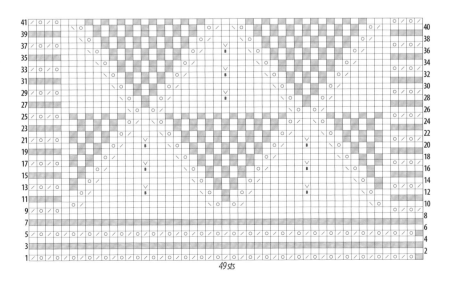

49 sts

Knitter's School

abbreviations

approx approximate(ly)
b in back of stitch
beg begin(ning)(s)
CC contrasting color
cn cable needle
cm centimeter(s)
cont continu(e)(ed)(es)(ing)
dec decreas(e)(ed)(es)(ing)
dpn double pointed needle(s)
foll follow(s)(ing)
g gram(s)
" inch(es)
inc increas(e)(ed)(es)(ing)
k knit(ting)(s)(ted)
LH left-hand
M1 make one
m meter(s)
MC main color
oz ounce(s)
p purl(ed)(ing)(s)
pat(s) pattern(s)
pm place marker
psso pass slipped stitch(es) over
rem remain(s)(ing)
rep repeat(s)
rev reverse(d)
RH right-hand
RS right side(s)
rnd round(s)
sc single crochet
sl slip(ped)(ping)
skp slip, knit, psso
ssk slip, slip, knit 2tog
st(s) stitch(es)
St st stockinette stitch
tbl through back of loop(s)
tog together
WS wrong side(s)
wyib with yarn in back
wyif with yarn in front
yd yard(s)
yo (2) yarn over (twice)

metrics

To convert the inches measurements used and in our instructions to centimeters, simply multiply the inches by 2.5.
For example: 4" x 2.5 = 10cm

Charts and symbols

Our charts show the right side (RS) of the fabric. In general, each "square" is a stitch; a row of squares represents a row (or round) of stitches. Heavy lines on the charts are used to define pattern repeats.
RS. When facing the RS of the fabric, read the chart from right to left as you work and work the stitches as the symbols indicate. If you are working circularly, work every round thus.
WS. If you are working back and forth in rows, every other row will be a wrong side (WS) row. Read WS rows from left to right as you work.

3-NEEDLE BIND-OFF

Uses. Instead of binding off shoulder sts and sewing them together.

Seam effect. Place *right* sides together, back stitches on one needle and front stitches on another. *K2tog (1 from front needle and 1 from back needle). Rep from* once. Bind first stitch off over 2nd stitch. Continue to k2tog (1 front stitch and 1 back stitch) and bind off across.
Ridge effect. Place *wrong* sides together, then work as above.

BACKWARD LOOP CAST ON

Uses To cast on a few sts for a buttonhole or the start of a sleeve. Form required number of backward loops.

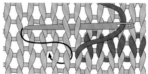

DUPLICATE STITCH

Duplicate stitch (also known as Swiss darning) is just that: with a blunt tapestry needle threaded with a length of yarn of a contrasting color, cover a knitted stitch with an embroidered stitch of the same shape.

STOCKINETTE GRAFT

1 Arrange stitches on two needles.
2 Thread a blunt needle with matching yarn (approximately 1" per stitch).
3 Working from right to left, with right sides facing you, begin with steps 3a and 3b:
   3a Front needle: yarn through 1st stitch as if to purl, leave stitch on needle.
   3b Back needle: yarn through 1st stitch as if to knit, leave on.
4 Work 4a and 4b across:
   4a Front needle: through 1st stitch as if to knit, slip off needle: through next st as if to purl, leave on needle.
   4b Back needle: through 1st stitch as if to purl, slip off needle: through next st as if to knit, leave on needle.
5 Adjust tension to match rest of knitting.

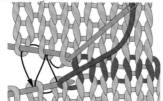

INTARSIA

When changing from one color to the next when working intarsia, it is necessary to twist the yarns to prevent holes. Pick up the new color from under the old color, as shown, and continue working.

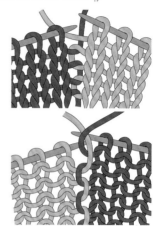

INVISIBLE CAST-ON

Uses As a *temporary cast-on*, when access to the bottom loops is needed: to knit, graft, attach a border, or for an elastic hem.

1 Knot working yarn to contrasting waste yarn. With needle in right hand, hold knot in right hand. Tension both strands in left hand; separate the strands with fingers of the left hand. Yarn over with working yarn in front of waste strand.

2 Holding waste strand taut, pivot yarns and yarn over with working yarn in back of waste strand.
3 Each yarn over forms a stitch. Alternate yarn over in front and in back of waste strand for required number of stitches. For an even number, twist working yarn around waste strand before knitting the first row.
Later, untie knot, remove waste strand, and arrange bottom loops on needle.

MAKE 1 KNIT (M1K)

Uses A single increase.

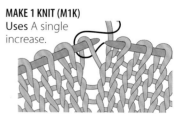

1 For a *left-slanting increase* (M1L), with right needle from back of work, pick